CW01391618

Out of the Shadows

KIM WYMER

Copyright © 2015 Kim Wymer

All rights reserved.

ISBN: 978-1508871408

DEDICATION

This book is dedicated to Kerry Wymer Davis, I will love you unconditionally for an eternity, with all my heart and soul.

FOREWORD

I am delighted and honoured to write the foreword to this book. Having gone through my own personal transformation, I thrive on empowering and witnessing others achieve the same. As I frequently remind people, it's no point *knowing* what to do, you must *do* what you know. We can hand people the 'tools' but if they don't pick them up and use them, their life is never going to change.

Kim Wymer is a wonderful inspiration to others. She made the decision to work on herself and change her thinking and her attitude to life. I strongly and firmly believe the greatest investment anyone can make is to look within and work on themselves. Our outer world is a reflection of what's going on in our inner world; our thoughts, emotions and attitude to life.

In this book, Kim gives a very frank and open insight into her life, the traumas and dramas and how on her journey she continues to experience a wonderful transformation.

Some people 'go' through life and other people 'grow' through life. This book celebrates our unlimited potential to grow, blossom and evolve – in spite of everything. It is a book of hope.

Kim is a valued member and Accredited Coach within the Sue Stone Foundation, whose mission is to spread positivity, happiness, success and love across the world. Through sharing and putting the tenets of our belief into action in our daily lives and utilising the amazing powers of the Universe, we can fulfill our aspirations of living our lives with love, compassion, understanding and fulfillment and reach our goal of inner peace, contentment and happiness.

As we attain inner peace for ourselves it will positively affect those around us and through the ripple effect it can eventually influence the entire world.

Sue Stone
the Sue Stone Foundation

CONTENTS

OUT OF THE SHADOWS

ACKNOWLEDGMENTS

Throughout my life there have been many people who, without their influence, it would never have been possible to make this book a reality.

I would like to thank my loving parents Melody and Bob for bringing me into this world and loving me unconditionally.

I would like to thank my two beautiful children, Jeri and Jake, for their love and support, for being understanding and helping me through all the difficult times in my life, I love you both so much.

I would like to thank my brother, Scott, and my sister-in-law, Julie, and all their wonderful children. My sister, Kerry, my brother-in-law, Steve, and their amazing children.

A special thank you to my nephew, Reece, for helping me compile, edit and structure all of the material for this book.

Thank you to my friend and mentor Sue Stone and all my friends and colleagues, old and new. Thank you for sharing this life journey with me, I love each and every one of you.

And thank you to John and Joey for putting me on this path, you have both taught me more valuable lessons than you could ever know.

PREFACE

We all live in our own bubbles, experiencing our own personal journey and only seeing the world through the lens of our own eyes. Another person could live in the same home as you for twenty years but still see life in a completely different way; viewing things that happen in a totally different light. Everyone's perception is slightly different - we are all unique individuals on a journey through life.

This is my life; this is how I saw it.

When asked, most people will say that you are who you are and nothing you or anyone else can do will change that. I am living proof that you are far more powerful than you believe and by utilising a positive mindset, even the most impossible tasks can be done. This is the story of how I went from a punked-out, borderline alcoholic with no direction in life, no goals or dreams outside of being a miserable housewife, to a confident, independent business owner with more to offer the world than I ever knew.

It wasn't until the second half of my life I realised that everything I'd been through up until that point; the fear and the loneliness, heartache and unhappiness, were lessons to be learned. All the people, events and scenarios I experienced, I had attracted to myself.

People came into my life, as they come into all of our lives, to teach us lessons that we must learn from.

I lived the first half of my life without knowing that I could have had a little more control over the things I went through just by asking for it. Now it's a different story. Since studying the Law of Attraction and discovering my own spirituality, I feel in control of my life. I have faith in myself and I trust in the power of the Universe.

My eyes are open and I'm more aware of life's bigger picture. I want to keep on learning - something my school-age self would probably slap me for saying. I want to love more, care more, give more and express myself in ways I would never have thought possible for me. I want to take the chances and opportunities I missed when I was too blind to see them, or too scared to take them.

I have learned so much and hope that in these pages I may just be able to help someone as other writers have helped me.

Part 1: John

1 EAST END GIRL

I was born on the 31st of January 1967 in Stepney, East London. My parents were only young themselves, but by the time I turned two I already had a younger brother and sister. We moved around a lot in my early years, from places like the Isle of Dogs to Dagenham, from houses to high-rise estates, where at five years old I could look out from the balcony of our 18th floor flat and see the entirety of London for miles and miles; the monotone expanse of concrete buildings stretching out like a large, grey field; the dullness of it only intersected by the muddy river Thames snaking through the city.

After having spent the early years of my childhood in the dingy gloom of the city, we packed up and moved out to Dagenham. At the time and in comparison to the Isle of Dogs, it was a paradise, where the sun shone against my skin and there was a lush, green garden to play in. It was overgrown and choked with weeds but it was full of creepy-crawlies, which I loved — especially spiders. I would scoop them up and keep them in matchboxes punctured with little air holes so that I could inspect them.

For as long as I can remember I had always been a quiet kid. I mostly stayed out of the way of trouble

,definitely wasn't one to get into fights with other kids outside of my family and in a way, I guess that made me an easy target.

On the next street over to us there lived a family who I made sure to stay clear of because one of the little boys was a mouthy smoker with a bad reputation. He would stalk the local streets with his deaf and mute brother and one day, on the way home from school, I noticed them coming towards me. I panicked and crossed the road, knowing that they were going to try to cause trouble; my heart caught in my throat when I saw them cross the road as well and I got ready to run, but the loud little boy grabbed me before I could.

"Quick, get her!" he shouted, and they pinned me to the floor. He kissed me hard and forcefully and with the two of them holding me I couldn't get him off. I tried to move my face away but his brother was holding my head down as well. Panic was rising in my throat, I wanted to kick and punch but the fear kept me paralysed. Eventually, they ran away laughing, leaving me lying on the concrete, my mind swimming with fury and shame. What had I done to deserve that? I was a quiet kid who kept to herself, and after that day I felt more alone and distant than ever. I never wanted to face something like that again, so I made sure to steer clear of any conflict I could from then on.

After a while of living in Dagenham, mum began to miss her family back in London, and although it was only a twenty minute drive to see them, we ended up moving back. Another mutual exchange and we were back in the city on a council estate in Mile End. The estate was huge, and all the maisonettes looked exactly the same, with every inch of floor space covered in square paving that gave it the look of a concrete jungle. The streets were littered with children, their playful shrieks rang through the air at every time of day and night and we were never short of kids to play with.

Opposite our house was a huge, old fashioned pub set back in a car park, called the Britannia. We were in the thick of the drunken patrons, which often included my parents and other neighbours, who would come flooding from the noisy building every night. To our left lay a row of shops, so we never needed to leave our enclosed little world, except to go to school.

Although I was quiet and reserved, I loved to play with the other kids, especially the boys. I would sit and laugh at their banter and try to jump from one shed roof to another, hopping along the back of the gardens in our street.

When the time came to pick the secondary school I wanted to attend, my friend who had already been there for a year, Kay, convinced me to forgo our local school and join the one she attended, twenty minutes away from where we lived. I agreed and we spent the entire summer hopping from roof to roof, laughing and playing without a care in the world. As the summer drew to a close, Kay informed me that she would be leaving Mile End and moving school. I was going to be completely alone in a school where I knew no one and I was shy enough as it was. Obviously, I was upset - who was going to look after me now? Funnily enough I don't even remember the day Kay left, I must have spent the whole day sulking.

I wore my school uniform for a week before school started; I thought I looked the nuts in it, with my long white socks and my smart black shoes that made a clip clopping sound when I walked.

When I came home from school I would still spend the evening jumping from shed roof to shed roof, and I made new friends on those roofs after Kay left - I even met my first best friend in the gang I knocked about with. Jenny was her name, she went to an all girls school in Mile End and seemed pretty clued up about things.

One of our first weeks in secondary school, we had to go on a trip to Wales, it was either that or endure a whole week of P.E, and my complete and utter lack of athleticism made it an easy choice. I kept to myself most of the trip and seemed to get on with the other girls, until a girl named Monique began to pick on me. Monique was loud, angry and had decided that I was to be her next target. The other girls flocked around her because if you weren't on Monique's good side, you were in for trouble.

I returned to the room I shared with Monique and five other girls one afternoon, to find that they had packed my bag and thrown me out of the room. Unfortunately, it didn't stop there, and even when we returned from Wales she would throw threats and abuse my way in her gruff, booming voice. Worry balled up in my throat every morning at the thought of having to go to school and face Monique, but my worry soon turned to anger. Why did this keep happening to me? What was I doing so wrong that kept attracting these people into my life? I was quiet and unconfident, but never nasty and malicious. I would run home from school every afternoon to punch my pillow in a fit of rage and sadness. *This is Monique's face*, I thought as I planted my fist into it again and again. The bullying had become so aggressive and happened so often that even older kids would tell her to leave me alone when they saw her throwing abuse at me.

"Just bloody hit her!" my dad and brother would urge. I was never a violent person but the idea of hurting her the way she hurt me every day became more and more appealing.

I endured Monique's vicious words every day for months and months, I began to think that I'd never escape her and that she'd follow me through the rest of my life, screaming cruel words at me in her booming voice, until a note was passed to me in a History class one day. *"Pass it to Wymer,"* I heard repeatedly as the note was passed through six other kids before it got to me.

"Monique says this is for you," the girl next to me whispered as she passed me the note.

My heart jumped into my throat when I read the words, *Let's fight* scrawled in her handwriting. I almost ran out of the class in tears, but I was sick of it, and sick of her. I hurriedly wrote an agreement on the note and wedged it back into the other girl's hand.

I left that class with a lump in my throat, but when I stepped outside Monique was nowhere to be found. Even in our next class she never met my eye, and when it came time to leave school that day, I dreaded the thought of her jumping me at the school gates. Still, she was nowhere to be found, and the next day when I asked a classmate what had happened, she told me that Monique just didn't want to fight me anymore.

From that day with Monique I knew the only way to stop myself getting picked on was to try to be braver; even if it was false bravado, I realised that keeping to myself and staying quiet would just get me walked all over even more.

So I began to rebel, in the only way I could, I dyed my hair and slapped some makeup on, and by the time I'd turned fifteen I was full on punk. I would spend ages spiking my hair up and picking out the best shade of black lipstick, because those things are so important for school. I still wasn't an aggressive person, but dressing like that meant I could draw attention to myself without having to actually say anything. I got noticed because of the way I dressed, and gained a bit of popularity. I'd even taken up smoking a year earlier, in a desperate bid to fit in and keep the bullies away.

"Meet you in the bog for a fag!" we'd say, and we'd all run to the girls toilets at break and lunch time and smoke ourselves silly, laughing and chatting about fashion, or boys we fancied. I really didn't like school, I failed most of my exams because I wasn't interested in the subjects and I never did study properly, honestly, I was more interested in bunking off lessons and hiding in the toilets to have a crafty cigarette.

I didn't want to learn because I was lazy minded, I would look at the work and tell myself *I don't get it; I can't be bothered*, and think about the next chance I would get to sneak off and have a cig.

I had a Saturday job during school, at our local pie mash shop, where we would clean the dishes from the tables and make cups of tea for the customers. After working there for a while I never wanted to eat the stuff again, but it paid me enough to buy cigarettes and spend my weekends getting off my face at the Britannia. No one cared about underage drinking back then, we were completely free to kill our developing bodies every weekend with alcohol and cigarettes. I'd leave my job at the shop and head home to get ready for the night.

At sixteen, I left school; my sister was fourteen and had been with her boyfriend a year already, and my brother was barely in the house, like most teenagers. I had no plans for college, because that was only for the posh kids; besides, I'd only managed to get an O Level in Art. I'd left school and all I had was my part time job in the pie shop and no career prospects, we'd still blow our wages getting pissed every Saturday night, of course, and I wasn't bothered by a career at that point anyway.

The January of 1984 was cold and bitter, even so I'd still stand outside my front door, just observing people as they came and went, but sometimes mates would stop by and chat. One day, stood outside the front door with my friend, Alice, I saw a man rush by. He looked flustered and seemed to be looking for someone; Alice recognised him and called out. Fonzie, she called him, and I could see why, he looked just like the *Happy Days* character, with his jeans, white tee and leather jacket. I'd seen him before with blonde girls on his arms, he had a lovely face and a good physique.

"Who are you looking for?" she asked him.

"Peter Jones and Laura Manning," he replied angrily "she's my girlfriend and I think she's carrying on with him."

Alice just waved him on, and he stalked off after his girlfriend.

A few days passed, and Alice came knocking again. "See Fonzie, he fancies you," she said grinning, "so I gave him your number."

"Alice, you didn't!" She only laughed herself silly. He was nice, but he was twenty-six and I wasn't even seventeen yet. She made a few jokes and laughed it off; I never thought he'd be interested in me anyway. I was basically still a school girl, still a child despite the heaps of make-up I piled on to my face. I was still a virgin, still shy and unconfident; still had no idea about men at all.

When he called, the conversation was short, and even over the phone I could feel my face burning with embarrassment. He told me that his name was John, and asked if he could take me out. I said yes, but that called up the question of how I was going to tell my parents. Somehow I plucked up the courage one night, and sat my parents down.

"Do you know Fonzie? You know, the one who drew Scott the Mickey Mouse, the artist bloke?"

"Oh yeah I know him, his dad drinks in the Brit, what about him?" dad asked.

"Dad, he rang and asked me out."

"He's older than you, isn't he?" he questioned.

"I think so..." I lied, knowing he was ten years older than me.

"I hear he's a nice quiet fella, are you going?"

"I dunno yet," I lied again. Thankfully, the age gap didn't seem to bother my parents much, and if he was known as quiet that was even better, because I was too.

2 IT'S ONLY HAIR

1987, and I'm twenty years old. Eastenders is playing on TV at home, and we were all glued to it. I remember two characters, Michelle and Lofty, were going to get married. Lofty had asked her to marry him, and she had jilted him at the altar. I thought about how harsh Michelle had been for letting him down on their wedding day, *Michelle, you cow, how could you do that to that poor man*? I remember thinking. Everyone at home was really getting into the drama of it all.

Michelle was using her gut feeling, her intuition, she was thinking of her own feelings and her own future, not his.

At this tender age of twenty, I was just about to get married myself, to a man named John I'd met three years prior.

John was good looking, cool and friendly. He was known as a nice, quiet guy, not one of the boozers who would waste their time hanging about in the pub; drinking, smoking and gambling all of their money away. He seemed a decent bloke and my parents approved of him. Most importantly, he showed an interest in me, and as someone who had no confidence in myself whatsoever (especially in front of men), that made me like him even more.

John had a nice car, which was definitely attractive to a young girl. We could go on adventures and drive around wherever we wanted. I loved it, we were free and it was exciting for me. Most boys my age were three years younger in the head and they would spend their time hanging around the streets at night not doing much at all. I felt a bit more grown up because my boyfriend had a car and a good, secure job.

My very first date with John was so nerve-wracking. Being a bit of a fashion freak, I wore a tonne of makeup, spiked my hair up as best as I could and wore my long khaki army coat and my big, black leather, buckle clad boots. I loved the punk-rock style and I thought I looked the business.

I got into John's car the night of our very first date; I noticed he had a pile of magazines on the floor. They were music magazines, NME specifically, and I was impressed that he was into his music just as much as I was. However, while I was into punk and alternative stuff like the Sex Pistols and the Clash, John's taste went right across the board from pop to classical, a bit more cultured than me, I thought. We drove around and didn't say much. I felt so shy; I could feel my face burning up with embarrassment.

A year later, we went on a weekend trip to Paris. I was so pleased; no one else my age was getting asked to go off to the most romantic city in the world. By then my fashion style was changing, because John liked to see me a bit more lady-like, more grown up with my fashion sense.

Sometimes when he came to visit I would still be in my dressing gown, my wet hair all wrapped up in a towel and I wanted to stay like that because I was comfortable, but John would get annoyed with me because I didn't dress up for him when he came over. In his eyes I was being a slob and not making an effort for him. I knew he didn't like the punk look I had either, so I gradually changed myself for him, and began to buy more mainstream clothes to make him happy. He had standards and he liked me to look nice.

So I went along with it, doing whatever it took to please him. My spiked black hair was dyed peroxide-white, and my punk clothes traded in for dresses and heels. I would become the image of femininity for him, even at the cost of the fashion that I loved so much.

Paris was so romantic though, and the hotel we stayed in was lovely and posh. Deciding that we should go up into the Eifel tower; a challenge considering John was claustrophobic and would not even get into a lift, we trundled up the stairs until we reached the top. Finally at the top, John pulled out a ring box and proposed to me. I was flabbergasted; I got embarrassed and blushed and said yes, but didn't really know how to appreciate it at the time. All I knew or cared about was that I had a sparkly ring. Thinking about the future was a foreign concept to me.

We lived with our parents and John desperately wanted to move out, so we put our names on the Council housing list and waited. John kept writing to the Council and all kinds of housing trusts, complaining all the while about how they had not given us a home yet. He did all the chasing around and I let him get on with it. He would make all the plans; I didn't have to do anything other than agree with him. I had no input, and frankly, no desire to have any. Letting John deal with all of this was easier for me. I have always been quite laid back; it's in my nature to go along with what others say because I never liked arguments or conflict. So John continued to write his letters, while I was excited about how I would decorate the place and which cat I wanted, and how I could finally have my own space.

At the time John was always so conscious of his hair and would always be putting dark dye gloo in it, he wouldn't even let me touch it. I could see it was beginning to thin out; I would tell him that it didn't bother me, but deep down it did. I felt sorry for him and for myself, I was nineteen and my fiancé was going bald, he was visibly devastated that this was happening to him. I was upset for him and selfishly upset for myself. What would people think? I worried what people would say, at the time I couldn't understand how he felt, at the time all I could think of was how I was too young to have a bald boyfriend.

I was getting snide remarks from people about our age difference which didn't help, but I just carried on because I felt sorry for him. He was my first real boyfriend and I didn't want to hurt him. So I tried to ignore the remarks, just pretending that I didn't hear them.

Sometimes when we went out we would get looked at. I remember in a pub one night a man said to me "What are you doing here with your dad?", and I felt terrible, but I never told John. I tried to put remarks to the back of my mind. I did love John, with what I thought was love. In the beginning it was lust which then got comfortable, and then you get used to each other. Then you say the words "I love you", because it feels nice and pleases the other person, but as time went on, I became less and less sure about our relationship.

I remember staying over at John's flat most weekends where he lived with his mum in Mile End and going home Sunday evening in floods of tears, crying because I was worrying about his hair loss. I had such mixed feelings about it, how could I end the relationship because of my own superficial expectations of how he should look? How could I be so heartless? The guilt would be unbearable. He seemed to dote on me, I was his everything, he didn't even have that many friends; his focus was all on me. If I broke up with him, what would he have left?

I got home to find my sister and her boyfriend there; they could see I had been crying, a regular occurrence for me. So I finally opened up to them and told them why, we all hugged each other and they tried to comfort me.

"Don't worry babe, it'll be okay. It's only hair, everyone has stuff wrong with them. No one's perfect," Steve told me.

I really tried to take on board what he was saying, it was true after all; besides, the thought that no one else would want me anyway, and that I'd be left on the shelf was always on my mind. I really didn't have any confidence in myself. So I made a decision to stay with John and try my hardest to make it look like his hair problem didn't bother me.

Time went by; one day John came to me and said that he had been to one of the housing trusts he'd be writing to, they'd had our names on the list for ages and because they were a Christian trust, we would be considered for a property to rent if we were married.

I had no intention of rushing into getting married so early in my life, besides, I definitely was not into pretty bridal gowns or wedding stuff at all, all that fluffing about, everyone focusing on the bride, me being the centre of attention. NO. WAY. It seemed too much, but the thought of moving out and having my own space was so tempting. So John asked me.

"What do you think, shall we get married then?"

I said yes.

"But please, no fuss."

3 GOING TO THE CHAPEL

No plans were made for the wedding, other than John going to the registry office to book a date.

"How does the 28th of March sound?" He asked. It was only two months after my twentieth birthday.

I said okay, and left it at that. He organised the lot and just asked me if that was okay, and I always said yes. I hated goal setting or plan making or anything that I had to lead with, it was sheer laziness and unwillingness.

We got married at Bow Registry Office, I never invited a single person to my own wedding, I just wanted a quick affair with just John and I, his mum and her partner and my parents.

After the usual stress of a bride trying to find her wedding dress, (I settled on a knee-length, white party dress with a runner of gold and white animal print in the front to match my large, curly perm that was more like straw than hair), my mum had bought me a lacy white umbrella for me to carry on the day, a dangly silver horse shoe and a lucky black cat like a traditional bride would hold.

On the 28th of March, my dad drove me to the registry office in his cab. It began to rain slightly; though it had been gloomy and wet all day. We pulled up and sat in the cab for a while, my heart was thumping rapidly against my chest. I could see so many people outside the office that I recognised, they were all John and I's family, this was the exact opposite of what I wanted. My nerves shot through the roof and I started shaking. Dad looked at me through the rear mirror,

"Are you okay, kid? Are you sure you want this?"

I gulped and stared back at him.

"I think so, yeah, Dad I'm okay." I thought back to Lofty and Michelle, and wondered if I should do the same and just not go in. I finally understood how difficult it must have been for Michelle to just leave. How could I disappoint all the people that had come to see the wedding? How could I show John up like that?

We went in anyway, and I gave them my biggest smile. Looking back, I know shouldn't have done it, I should have just driven away, but all I could think was how could I let him down? How could I be that heartless? He would be devastated, and I could see his sorrowful face just looking down at his feet. I would have let all the other people down, my parents, his family; the effort they all went through to prepare for this day. How selfish would that be of me to let everyone down? I just did not want to feel the guilt of everyone pointing at me, jeering "you bloody wicked cow", like I did when Michelle left Lofty.

I was thinking of everyone else, their feelings and not my own. I would have to live with that, and then I would definitely be left on the shelf. No one would want me. Why did I do this to myself? Why did I not use my intuition in the first place when we first met? I never did speak up, ever. At the time I didn't yet know how that one small decision, how getting out of that cab instead of driving away, would domino through the next twenty years of my life, like a bullet through a thousand sheets of glass.

I had done it, I had got married; got the little flat and the fluffy cat I had always wanted, and rent only cost £20 a week. Things were good for a while, John and I would tell each other that we loved one another, but over time it got less and less. I don't think I knew what love was at that young age. I deeply regret not being open and honest and talkative, it's a big lesson I have learned in life. I never actually said what I really deeply meant for fear of hurting people's feelings. I would hide my true feelings, I'd suppress and smother them and feel silly expressing them.

At home, John paid for everything; the rent, the bills and the food shopping. My money was my own and I just squandered it. I never paid for living there; I just worked in a library and did a bit of housework now and then.

A few years passed and I found out, unexpectedly, that I was pregnant. I ballooned up to a fair old size and I suffered with leg swelling, all the usual glamour that accompanies pregnancy. I was definitely a water carrier, a typical Aquarian, and I gave birth to a beautiful baby girl. I gave up my library job because I wanted to bring up my own child and bond with her properly as a mother; I was quite content to not work and be a stay-at-home mum.

What made it all the better was that six weeks later my sister, Kerry, gave birth to a baby girl as well, this was fantastic, my best friend and I having our children together; spending lots of time together; growing together, it was great. Our children were best friends too, and we were so happy. Having our children together definitely made us bond much better as sisters, we became closer and we would laugh all the time, I really loved my sister's 'mad as a hatter' personality. We would be laughing so much over silly things that we would either cry or wet ourselves. But as I grew closer to my sister, my relationship with John began to feel more and more strained.

In our twenties, every now and then we would go out to pubs and then on to a club. We would get all dressed up, wear tons of make up and do our big fat perms as frizzy as we could. John didn't like me going out, he had a jealous streak that often reared its ugly head and I hated that. Coming home I would be bombarded with questions.

"Where did you go? Who were you with? Did you meet anyone? Did you dance with anyone?" I even remember him once saying, "Don't lie to me because I know where you go! I have spies!"

Yes I did speak to men, we all did, it was just called chatting and having fun with new people in the world, but I never told him that because I didn't want the animosity it would cause between us. Lying to keep the peace was not something I was opposed to, especially now that we had a child.

I look back now and think to myself *why was I like that? Why could I not be honest with him?* So what if he shouted at me? I could have shouted back and we could sort it out, but no, I stayed quiet. I absolutely loved going out with my sister and our friends, and sometimes even our mum would come out too. We would have a great time and not once did we ever go off with other men, we were young mums; we were a family and we would all stick together. I still absolutely loved to party and drink, and partook in both often, but John was not very sociable. He did drink at home but as for going out with friends, he never did. He only liked and wanted my company, though I began to realise my sister was my best friend and I valued her company more than John's. He made my life easy, but I was ten years younger and I wanted to have fun when he wanted to settle down.

Over time I began to realise I was not truly happy, but I stayed in the relationship out of a weird mix of compassion and fear. The years were passing and we both got on with our boring, daily routines, yet as we got older we were also changing, we were growing different in our thinking habits, we had different personalities and different styles, interests and attitudes. It made me think of how we got together in the first place.

Now and then he would ask me if I loved him, and I would give an obligatory "'Course I do," but I knew deep down it wasn't true, unconditional, soul-mate love. Not on my part anyway.

I fell pregnant again a few years later, and my beautiful son was born in the March of 1995. I was twenty-eight years old and John thirty-eight, and by the time my son was two I was feeling unhappier than ever inside. The same Groundhog Day routine, every single day: being a mother and a housewife to a man I didn't really love, over and over and over again.

A little while after my son was born I decided it was time to go back to work. I managed to secure a job in a local supermarket every Sunday, though this meant that my Saturday night party days were long gone. The housing trust that had given us our first place had introduced some scheme that would help people get on the property ladder, and we received a grant to help toward the deposit of our first home.

We decided on a three bedroom house in Essex, mid terraced, on the outskirts of Greater London. It was a nice little house, despite all the unsightly Artex, and it was ours. It had lofty ceilings and a little door looking out onto our lovely, long garden. Trees overarched into it, their leafy arms dipping onto the grass. The children had a space to play and John and I finally had the little place of our own that we'd always wanted, mostly we were just glad to get out of the hideous grey of the city.

Even though I was glad we had a good home for our children, the unhappiness I had begun to feel still festered inside me. Now that we had the mortgage and the kids, my selfish mind told me I was trapped now. I would look at John and focus on his bad side, it was so easy to overlook his good qualities and only see what I didn't like about him, and it was dragging me down even more. What with the monotony of the same routine day in day out really kicking in as well, I began to feel extremely, mind numbingly brain dead.

The only time I felt a bit better was when my family came over to see us. My brother, Scott, and sister in law, Julie, and their kids; my mum and dad and my sister and her family, they were so much fun. We would all have a drink and the beer and wine would flow and I played happy families for the night. John had four brothers and a sister and they hardly ever came over, we would only occasionally go to see them. Mine was a close knit family, who would hug and kiss when we met, my parents brought us up like that, to be loving and to show love, I was like this with my friends and family but not really with my husband. I lived with him in the same house and we had different ways of dealing with stuff, we both thought we were right in our ways of thinking, and we clashed because of it, I hated his attitude and he was probably frustrated with mine.

We were bought up entirely differently, in totally different environments, with totally different parenting and different mind programming. My family was loving and close-knit, John's were distant and never seemed to show their love like we did. He had lots of brothers but they were a lot older than him and they had left home when John was young, so he felt like an only child. His father was an abusive alcoholic and John had to live in this environment alone; he would often tell me terrible stories of the abuse his mother endured from his drunken father, until they finally broke up.

Every chance I could I would go out and visit my family, I'd take the kids to them and just loved to get out. Unlike John I was not the kind of person to watch a lot of TV, and my family's company made me feel good, the atmosphere was great, and we would have a good laugh. John rarely, if ever, came with me because he was tired from work, wanted to do more work on the house, or watch his TV programmes.

Even though John and I had our problems, he was still a doting and dedicated dad, and as our kids grew up he clung to them as if they were the apples of his eye. He made sure they always came first with everything, every week they would get a new toy or new clothes or shoes or whatever they wanted. They never went without love, toys, attention, playing, he would always make time for them. They have always been his world, and all our married life they came before me. My dad used to say a man should always put his wife first, because the kids fly the nest and then you're left with your wife forever, but it's not like that with everyone. Unfortunately, we continued to grow apart, though more so on my part, I didn't like John's ways, his opinions, his negativity or him as a person, quite frankly. Every time he expressed an opinion or moaned about something he was pushing me further and further away. It seemed that John was an expert complainer and it was like second nature for him. Of course, I'm not saying I never moaned, we all do; it's a form of communication. However, it seemed that as he got older he was doing more complaining than ever before. No topic was above moaning about; his job, the government, the TV shows he loved so much, the news, the weather, other people's lives. It was getting ridiculous.

I never spoke up and really told him how I felt because I just didn't want to fix us. I was going off of him on a daily basis, and I couldn't see his good side even if I tried. Maybe he moaned for attention, because I gave him none. I constantly wished that he would run away and leave me because I wasn't strong or brave enough to do it, besides; I had nowhere to go, and a crap job, so we plodded on.

How could I split up this family? No, I couldn't. I would devastate everyone. I thought of the upset it would cause to everyone and how it would spiral out of control. I imagined my kids and I out on the streets, my parents' disappointed faces; John having even more panic attacks.

I can't do this because it's the wrong time of year, I'd tell myself, among a myriad of other excuses I churned out to try to keep us together, mainly for the children. I completely and utterly blamed John for my unhappiness, but relationships go both ways, it was my fault as well for not speaking my truth and not speaking up, not dealing with our challenges there and then.

I remember feeling so low that I kept telling everyone that I thought I had Seasonal Affective Disorder syndrome, a disease where you feel low because of the cold, grey weather and the early nights, I just wanted to curl up all winter and hide from the world and only come out when it was nice and bright and warm again. Of course, I had to carry on because we had children to think of and a mortgage that John worked hard for. I was ashamed to say that the man I had married was depressing me because it was my choice to marry him and I chose the wrong man, I had made a bed of barbed wire and now I'd have to sleep in it.

I had attracted this man to me, or we attracted each other because we were on the same vibration at the time we met. The kids were growing up fast and the marriage routine was still pretty mundane. I was telling lies to keep it sweet because I could see no way out; I totally focused on the problems instead of focusing on the solutions.

I can only assume that John saw a miserable cow, which was reflecting on him, and the only time we got a bit amorous was on a Friday night after a good drinking session, when we didn't have to get up for work in the morning. We all need satisfying sexually to release tension, that's how I saw it, but because I never fancied my husband, I would close my eyes.

4 NU-METAL, NU-ME

When my son was about seven or eight years old, I decided I really wanted to get back into rock music again; because nu-metal was on the scene, bands like Linkin' Park, Limp Biskit and Papa Roach, I absolutely loved that sound. It was so cool and it made me feel good, it picked me up, it was fast and upbeat and exciting, I was *completely* obsessed. It took me back to my younger days when I felt free, and I just loved the alternative scene, the punk, the metal and the gothic. It just appealed to me at that time, because that was how I was feeling, dark and slightly angry. I was beginning to change again even at the age of thirty-five. The music took me to another world, and I would be glued to MTV2, Kerrang and Scuzz TV all day. It was a more upbeat, younger and updated metal scene, and I admit I latched on to it all for dear life, it seems strange but it was my outlet. I was not growing older gracefully; I was reverting back to my youth because I'd missed out on it all.

Even though I did get a few odd comments about the new, young metal scene and my age, I just did not care, this was my bliss at the time, my attitude became "why be a sheep and follow everyone else, why not be different?"

So I got back into my rock music, changed my clothing style as well, which I knew John really didn't like, but I was caring less and less about his opinions. Over time my whole wardrobe became a sea of black fabric, to match the mood I was in most of the time, and it suited my overweight physique. I would buy t-shirts with my favourite rock bands names on, paint my nails black and I even dyed my hair black, much to my husband's displeasure.

I became the antithesis of my sister, she always looked so pretty, with lovely hair and makeup and gorgeous clothes, like a lovely modern woman who was fashion conscious. She looked after herself and she was also really clever on the sewing machine, so she would also make some of her own clothes to suit her style; she was immaculate in my eyes and always happy. One particular day she strolled into my kitchen, we exchanged our usual cuddles and 'I love yous' and chatted until John came in..

"Wow you look nice," he said to her, "you always look great, very feminine, like a real woman should look." He turned to me and continued, "Why don't you ever look nice like your sister?"

She got slightly embarrassed, but we laughed it off, it was a simple comment but that's when I knew I was affecting him, I was pissing him off, and that felt good. I wanted to do everything in my power to put him off me, in the hopes that he would just leave. I wanted him to dislike me so much that he would go find a lovely, feminine lady to look after him and show him the love that I couldn't.

I really needed to get out of the house as much as I could so that I didn't have to sit in and watch boring repeats of *Only Fools and Horses, Alf Garnet* and *Victor Meldrew* playing over and over, I couldn't stand it anymore, so I tried to find an outlet, but had no idea what I was interested in other than my music.

Until one evening my neighbour knocked at my door and asked me to come in and take a look at her kitchen cupboards that she wanted to paint, because she had bought herself a pot of paint and grain effects paint. My neighbour had tried a couple of times and said that she messed it up and she just couldn't do it correctly.

"Would you have a go?" she asked.

So I had a go and I absolutely loved it, I didn't even need to concentrate on it, it just flowed, and created a gorgeous wood grain and wood knotting effect. She was pleased with the result, and I was very pleased with my efforts, which gave me a buzz I hadn't felt in a long time. It finally twigged that I might be able to make something out of this. I began looking in the yellow pages for adult courses on painting and decorating, and soon after a friend suggested I go to the library because they have prospectuses on adult education courses. I was so excited at the prospect of actually educating myself and doing something I was interested in, the big bonus, however, was being able to get out of the house. I thought about it all the time, it was me taking a bit of control over my life, and doing something with myself, I was tired of being the brain dead housewife I'd become.

So off I went to the library to find a prospectus, and I came across an interesting looking course called "*Specialist Paint Effects*", which taught the basic use of watercolour emulsions to create specialist colour effects such as rag rolling, sponging, colour washing and even marble effects. This seemed to be just what I was looking for, so I booked myself onto the course, and I absolutely loved it. It was a shame that it was only one night a week, I would have been prepared to go every night; I was in paint heaven.

Then a year later I enrolled on the follow-up course; *Advanced Specialist Paint Effects*, which was much more complicated because now chemicals were involved and it was very messy and smelly, but the effects were amazing, especially the wood graining effects. It blew me away, and

I became a real paint nerd, I felt that I had actually achieved something. For the first time since giving birth to my children, I felt proud of myself.

When I came home to show my work to my family, no one really seemed bothered with my efforts, so I kept it to myself, which dampened my spirit a lot. From then on I wanted to paint everything in sight. I would paint my furniture at home and do it over again when I got bored with it; I would even paint for family and friends for free because I loved it so much. People would say to me, "Why don't you do this for pay? You're good at it." To which I would simply reply a quick "No, no I'm not that good." I would completely doubt my capabilities, I wasn't trusting in myself and I would give myself negative self talk and tell myself I wasn't of a high enough standard to be charging, that it was just a hobby; *I'm only good enough to work for a supermarket, besides, no one would be interested anyway.*

I completely scared myself by imagining the worst things that could happen, instead of thinking of my boundless possibilities. I think a lot of people do that, maybe because we don't get enough encouragement at a young age, and that self doubt bleeds through into our adult lives. As Henry Ford once said, "*If you think you can or if you think you can't, either way you're right.*"

5 THIRTY-SIX GOING ON TWENTY-FIVE

My love for my nu-metal music continued to grow. On the weekends it was me, vodka and metal. I wanted to go and see all the lively new bands that everyone else was put off by. No one would come with me, I even offered to pay for their tickets, but I was obviously on my own here. Even my sister would say "Ooooh, no Kimmy, it's a bit much for me!"

I would eventually convince my brother to join me, and take him off to see my favourite bands, none of my friends or family liked the music, but Scott was an Oasis fan and didn't mind some of my music, so he was my only chance of actually getting to feel the buzz of seeing my favourite bands live. Excitement ran through my body like electricity, I felt so buzzed about getting a chance to crowd surf, it was what I loved, and no one could stop me. Bullet For My Valentine, Avenge Sevenfold, Disturbed and The Distillers, they had negative names and they sang negative words, angry words that expressed how they were feeling and I could relate to them. My own anger and confusion and negativity was propelling me towards this music.

The day of my first show with my brother, I felt like a teenager. I couldn't even remember the last time I was that excited, probably due to the blur of my brain cells being popped by the copious amounts of vodka and wine each night.

My daughter even said she would come along; the day could not come quick enough, to travel to London and actually see the band of the century that I was obsessing over. The day came and I couldn't even eat where I was so hyper, my daughter was twelve years old and her nutty mother was taking her to see her first rock band, but she was safe with me and my brother, as I promised myself not to drink on this occasion, not with my baby with me.

We arrived and we were right at the back of the stadium, so far away that the singers were hardly visible, they seemed like they were an inch high, but we had a brilliant time. And from then on I was forever planning my next gig, who could I convince to come with me next time? Definitely not John, he hated it. I would be upstairs in the house with my music on and he would be downstairs doing whatever he liked to do.

My mum was a sociable lady with lots of friends, and she would often go swimming at her local leisure centre. One day she got chatting to one of the pool attendants, a lady called Kelly. Kelly was covered in tattoos and her hair was dyed a vibrant red. My mum told her that I was into rock bands, tattoos, piercings and the whole gothic scene as well, and Kelly said that she would like to meet me because she had been looking for someone around her age to go to gigs with as well.

So we connected and I arranged to book us tickets to see a band called System of a Down, they were great and we became fast friends. We went to see a few bands after that and always had a great laugh, but she was a bit rough around the edges and much tougher than me; no one messed about with her, she even claimed to have had fights with grown men, which scared me a bit, so I made a conscious effort not get too close to her. I was at an angry time in my life, and perhaps that was why I attracted Kelly to me. We would just text each other now and then, but I knew I had to back off, I didn't want to go to a gig and leave with less teeth than I'd entered with.

Aged thirty-six I didn't think I looked my age. I never had any lines on my face and I was a smallish size in weight, because I did more drinking alcohol than eating food; in my head I looked and felt younger than I was. I must have driven John to despair with my raucous music, but I didn't even care; even my kids liked the music because the thrashing beats filled our house constantly. I was twenty-five in my bubble and this kept me alive, or at least gave me something to focus on.

Part 2: Joey

6 AN INNOCENT THOUGHT

After returning from a holiday in Australia, my sister began talking about emigrating, and every time I saw her she would go on about it like it was her obsession, but I was going deaf to her because that meant that she would be leaving me and I couldn't see that in my mind. I couldn't believe that something like that could be true. She was living a dream that wouldn't happen for her because I didn't want it to happen. She wouldn't do this to me or my parents, not my best friend. I'd look for any chance to change the subject every time it came up. After all, we had brilliant fun at her house most weekends, my brother in law was a joker and so was my sister. All our children were very close as cousins, and we all lived for each other. It was a very lively home, always something going on, and people were always visiting because they were very sociable people and they had a lot of friends. Why would she ever want to leave all that behind?

While my sister dreamt of a better life in Australia, I never thought of my future goals. I never had any; my brain was ignorant and numb. I didn't know what I wanted other than my music, my kids and my sister.

The one goal I did have was my mission to get John to leave me. His attitude was sucking the energy from me and I was caring less and less about my appearance and my attitude. I wanted him to look at me in disgust and just leave me alone, it wouldn't have bothered me one bit to be a single mum, because I was with the wrong man. I did everything I could to put him off me, from drinking too much to smoking cigarettes, which he hated. It must have been working, because by now it was rare for us to even be in the same room together. All I wanted was for him to come home one day and tell me he's leaving, that he'd found another woman, a normal, pretty forty-eight year old who would be more on his level.

I was getting bored at home and I needed money of my own, some spare cash, I was still only working one day a week at the supermarket, so I asked the manager if there was any overtime available in any department. I'd covered most departments over the years so I knew I'd have no problem in any of them.

I had many friends at work, of all ages and nationalities, a big melting pot of different people confined in the space of one building, which was great because I loved to hear about their different cultures and identities. It opened my eyes to the world at large. I had never had the chance to travel the world, but the whole world was in that supermarket.

Out of the blue, my boss offered me some overtime during the week and I agreed. So on the Monday I went into work, and it felt good, I felt like I had a purpose and I was going to earn a bit of spare cash. The day came and went and then I came in for a few more days here and there, then again the following week, and I actually began to look forward to it. It was a social place and it cheered me up. I was beginning to feel good about myself, I could go to work, have a laugh and get paid, and it got me out of the house.

One day I came in, entering the delicatessen as usual, and I noticed we had some new staff next door in the bakery. A new guy I had not seen before was standing there; I had to look twice at him because he was a big built man with big shoulders; a stocky frame and a wide chest, with the most angelic face and crystal blue eyes I had ever seen. My stomach fluttered uncomfortably. As I took in more about him I noticed his fair hair was spiked and he had that alluring punk-rock look about him, with tattoos creeping up his forearms just like the nu-metal men I was admiring on TV. In my eyes he was gorgeous, and I thought about how rare it was to see a good looking man working in a place like this, an innocent thought.

I was hit with a wave of disgust, how could I have the cheek to look at another man when I had been married for eighteen years? I wanted John gone more than anything but I could never cheat on him, I wasn't that sort of person.

I was setting up the deli one afternoon as the new guy walked past, a cheeky grin shot my way and I felt myself turn red, which he must have noticed. I couldn't help but laugh stupidly. He walked past a few more times and I pretended not to notice him, but I was well aware of his presence. He gave me butterflies, and while in my head I knew it was wrong, I couldn't help my feelings.

This went on for a few days; it was getting childish and ridiculous now. Why could I not just say hello to him? I was friendly enough to everyone else. I had forgotten how good butterflies in my stomach felt, that buzz inside that you can't control; my feelings only dampened when I snapped from my schoolgirl daze and realised who I was actually married to. I was a married woman and a mother, and I would just have to ignore this. I would tell myself off, but the other side of me was yearning for the butterflies to continue. Every time I saw him on the shop floor he was chatting to someone and they were cracking up laughing, not only did he look good but he was funny as well, which made it even more difficult to keep myself quiet.

It wasn't until I was tidying up the cheese counter with my back to the shop floor, I suddenly looked around and bouncing towards me was this guy. His name was Joey, I had discovered, but you would have been hard pressed to find a member of staff there who didn't know his name. I had also discovered that he was sixteen years younger than me. He was the centre of attention and his name was thrown around every two seconds by people trying to get his attention so that they could have a laugh and a joke with him. I thought constantly about how much fun he would be to talk to, and there he was looking at me.

"I can't believe it, my mate has just got me tickets to see Bullet For My Valentine!" he blurted out. He was smiling from ear to ear and I could feel his excitement radiating from him.

"Oh my God, you jammy git, how lucky are you!" I replied. That was our ice breaker, my way in.

Joey seemed to be everywhere I was, I began to notice he was having his breaks at the same time as me, and we would all go into the staff room and smoke ourselves stupid, puffing on as many cigarettes as we could possibly get into our lungs before it was time to go back to work. He was so funny, with his razor sharp wit and sarcastic sense of humour, there were few topics that he wouldn't crack a joke at. I couldn't wait until we had our breaks again so we could have a laugh; what with his good looks and his sense of humour, the vibes he was giving out were amazing and it made me feel so happy.

I was getting offered lots of overtime at work, and though I never wanted to work there permanently, the more I worked the more I saw Joey, and the more I got to know him the more I wanted him, even though he was only twenty-two and I was married. This was unthinkable, it was wrong, but my feelings took over me, this bright spark of a person made me feel on top of the world, made me feel alive. He was like a magnet, and I could tell he liked me too.

While I formed this amazing connection with this exciting man who seemed to be right on my wavelength, John and I were passing each other at home. No words were spoken between us, no connection, no excitement and no love, just the same as it had always been. I still spent a lot of my time upstairs, smoking and watching Kerrang, while he spent his time downstairs watching the news; the kids would pass between the both of us or be playing in the garden.

This is not how a marriage should be, I'd tell myself.

We both made no effort, any time we did talk it seemed like we were shrugging our shoulders and not really caring. We both liked a moan and a whinge, and it was becoming a habit on both parts, but to listen to John's negative comments felt like an iron bar constantly hitting me in the face. I was fed up and I never knew what he was thinking, but sometimes he would like to reassure himself and ask me if I still loved him. I would say yes to shut him up, when really I wanted to say no, to scream no, but I couldn't bring myself to do it. I gave him false hopes, and maybe he hated me because deep down he knew I was lying to his face every time he asked me.

Sometimes my niece would come over to stay at our home in the holidays because we had a big garden and they could be free and play outside safely. One Sunday evening John had to get up for work the next day and went to bed early. It was getting late and the girls were giggling when they went to bed, as children do, and they couldn't settle. They were kids and they loved to laugh, so I tried my best to keep them quiet and make sure they wouldn't wake up John. I went in to tell them off numerous times, but being kids this was even funnier to them and their laughter was louder each time.

It only took a few more times for John to erupt.

"*BLOODY SHUT UP!*" John would shout through the wall. I got back in bed and everything went quiet for a while as the girls seemed to have settled down. The negative energy radiating from John kept me awake, and sure enough the giggling soon started again.

John woke up in a rage, screaming at me to shut them up. In his anger I felt his foot come into contact with my stomach. We had taken to sleeping at opposite ends of the bed, and the strength of his kick forced the wind from my body as I rolled over in pain. Was that aimed at me? Would I have been hit if I hadn't been at the other end of the bed? I didn't know. I jumped out of bed in the dark and stood up, my breathing fast and heavy and thick with anger. I was angry at the girls and at John and at myself for being so weak, for not having the guts to say what I wanted to say.

"You fucking kicked me." My belly throbbed from the impact. "*You fucking kicked me!*" were the only words I could muster.

A vision flashed in my mind's eye, I was holding the pillow over John's face, holding it down and not letting go. I wanted to slam his face against the headboard and leave him lying there, or grab him by the throat and let out all my rage. I knew I had to get out of there, to stop the anger swilling around in my brain from making me do something I'd regret.

I stormed from the room, raced downstairs in a rage; lit a cigarette and tried to calm down. As the acrid smoke rose lazily around me, I knew my feelings of hatred toward John had never felt this strong. I hated him with a passion, and it was giving me the fire I needed to go on. I thought of Monique and those boys that had attacked me and how angry they must have been, they must have felt like I did, but just didn't have the self control to just walk away.

After that night things seemed to spiral out of control, the hateful vibes we gave off to each other seemed to rebound and multiply.

I couldn't wait to go back to work and see my friends and Joey, the guy who made me laugh, who made me feel happy and good about myself, the one who had started to compliment me and take an interest in me. With everything we had in common and his amazing personality, I could feel myself getting fonder of Joey as I drifted from John.

It felt so good, but so wrong at the same time, and it didn't seem to bother him that I was older, so I tried my hardest to push our ages to the back of my mind. I started to respond to him; when he asked for my number under the guise of wanting to text me if any gigs came up, I gave it to him. There was nothing in it, just a text. So every now and then we'd send a silly joke or picture, like you do with your mates, and that was all it was for a while. My face would light up when I saw his name on my phone, and pretty soon we began to talk over the phone instead of through text.

Joey's attitude to life was so laid back and he seemed so intelligent, really grown up for his age. He said all the right things and it seemed like everything he said was exactly what I was thinking, like he understood me. He gave me sensible advice when I asked for it, and I remember wondering where all this was coming from. We could have adult conversations about life and I couldn't believe how on my level he was. He seemed wise, or was I just naive? I felt young at heart, so maybe we met half way at some place only we knew existed.

We gradually started to talk about our families, and I told him about my children, while steering the conversation away from John whenever he came up. He told me about his parents and how they split up when he was young; about his mum who had a few life challenges with alcohol, and how he had been bought up by his Nan and still lived with her to look after her, and I really felt for him. He really had been through some challenges at such a young age, which explained his wise-beyond-years demeanour. Then his age would pop into my head again and I would feel wrong for a while, though it didn't take much to throw this thought to the back of my mind.

One particular day, sitting at home as was usual on a day off, the sound of nu-metal blasting through the TV speakers, I saw my phone light up. *Joey*, flashed across the screen in bright letters. He had sent me a text to invite me to go and see a band at a pub in Ilford, and mentioned that maybe a couple of friends from work might come along too. I thought about how John would react, and jokingly replied telling him that John would probably kill me if he found out. Straight away I knew I should not have said it, because now I'd just confirmed to him that I was interested. However, the idea started to play on my mind. *Shall I go? No, I can't, it's wrong, what if John found out?* It took a while for me to convince myself that going might be a good idea, telling myself that I'll go because I can have any friends I want. It's my choice; he's only a mate. Anyway, others from work would probably be there too and I really wanted to go.

It took me a few weeks to decide and it was all I could think of. Joey was on my mind a lot, his lovely face; his charming personality and his big build. I got butterflies just thinking about what that night might be like.

As weeks went by I kept hearing his name more than usual; his name was mentioned on the radio when the DJs were giving dedications, on the TV and in the papers. I would hear his name in people's conversations and my friend even sent me a joke in a text with his name in it. I couldn't help wondering what was going on. Where was all this coming from? Am I meant to go to this pub or what? It felt like magic as confusion and excitement bubbled in my stomach. Little did I know that this was due to my thoughts of Joey being sent out into the universe and, like a magnet, coming straight back to me. What you give out you get back, like attracts like and I was thinking of this guy a lot.

So I followed these signs and decided to go, reasoning that it was only a drink in a pub, no harm done. I told John I was going out with my mates from work; I had never lied to him like this before, telling my husband that I was meeting friends when really I was meeting another man; a man that I liked. I knew that he wouldn't appreciate me having male friends; he was quite old school like that, so I wanted to avoid that confrontation altogether. Luckily, John never questioned me, he was used to me going out and I don't think he cared anyway; he probably disliked me as much as I did him.

So the day came and out I went. I punked myself up as nu-metal chic as I could, which was normally head to toe black clothing. I wore my black satin pencil skirt, my big spiky biker boots with a lady-like heel and buckles up the side, a small black tee with my favourite band on it and a tiny black waist coat.

I got to the pub and stepped out of the cab into the crisp night air. Nervously, I walked toward the building. I would not go in alone, no way, I wasn't that brave. So I waited until a cab pulled up and Joey came bowling out of it by himself. My heart went over and I felt sick with nerves, I couldn't believe I was actually meeting another man for a drink; I promised myself I wouldn't drink too much and I would definitely be going home when the pub closed. *I'm not easy, I'm not like that.* Besides, I wasn't going to raise any suspicion with John at home by strolling in at nine o'clock the next morning.

The band was brilliant and we chatted and laughed. Joey was complimenting me left right and centre, I couldn't take them at all because I wasn't used to getting compliments, so every now and then I'd spit a sarcastic retort along the lines of "Yeah right!" or "Shut up!"

That night I had a lot to drink, the vodkas were flowing, and my nerves eventually calmed down. *What the hell am I doing?* I continued to ask myself, despite how much fun I was having. Me, a married mother, in a rough, punk pub with a man sixteen years younger than me, I almost couldn't believe my own life.

I was so bloody bored and fed up and dissatisfied with my home life, and my husband, and the hum drum routine, I felt smothered by the nothingness of it all. I was ready to explode and take a risk for once, I'd just take the consequences as they came; I didn't care anymore. I wanted to rebel again; I wanted to take a risk just this once, just for the buzz. The drink was fuelling me, and I wanted some well deserved excitement for once. I was numb and all I could think was *I don't bloody care anymore!*

I was loving it, and I didn't want it to end, I wanted more. The pub band played their last song and we left, waiting outside for the parade of cabs that would streak down the road and line up along the pavement, ready to cart the hoard of inebriated patrons home. I had pre-booked my cab to get me at around eleven; the night was cold but the atmosphere between Joey and I was hot and thick and syrupy, and as I leaned in to say goodbye, we kissed. This was no run of the mill, ordinary goodbye peck between friends, this was passionate and exciting; something I hadn't had in a long, long time. It was heaven, and I felt the intoxication of vodka and excitement. Soon enough, however, my cab came to drag me away from the fun.

7 DON'T YOU LOVE ME ANYMORE?

After that night, Joey was all I could think of, I was obsessed by now and I told not a soul, not even my sister. It was our secret, I stressed that we were to tell no one, it was just a one off, an innocent fling, but in reality it was what I had wanted desperately for years now.

My home life was a joke, my marriage was non-existent, but thankfully the kids were okay, their happiness seemed to be the one thing John and I could agree on, and they knew nothing of our sad marriage. It was normal for them to see us as two separate people living in one home.

I began to find it easier and easier to lie to John. One evening I told him I was with friends at work but I wasn't, instead I was with Joey. I had finally found someone to talk to, to confide in, someone who could provide decent conversation and some passion. We could pour our hearts out to each other and he seemed to really understand me, I guess he could relate to having been handled a rough deal in life. It felt so good to get things off my chest with someone who wasn't going to judge me, someone who *wanted* to be with me; someone who would lift my mood so high I was flying. We laughed all the time, and I wanted him more and more, this fling that was supposed to be a one off was getting heavier and heavier. We would text each other at night when everyone had gone to bed until the early hours of the morning. John was used to me not going to bed with him anyway, and when I did I would make sure he was asleep and sleep at the bottom of the bed, or get in with my kids.

The arguments between John and I became so frequent that looking back, I couldn't tell one from the other. I left the house in a rage one night and took the kids over to my sister's home, where I was free to sit and slag John off all night. I told her how I was not getting on with him, which she knew anyway, and how I couldn't stand him any longer. I suppose she had been expecting an outburst like this one of these days, but I always did my best to keep my feelings to myself and try to hide the fact that my marriage was a complete and utter shambles. Unfortunately, my sister was not blind.

That night my daughter stayed at my sisters and my son slept in the car on the way home. Driving back home I was miserable, but I had a CD of one of my favourite bands at the time, Evanescence, playing through the speaker. The goth-pop diva's voice filled the car, and every now and then a song would skip. One song kept on jumping at the part where she sings "*I don't love you anymore.*" It was loud, it seemed louder and then it stopped and my head filled with a strange and stagnant silence, all I could hear was "*I don't love you anymore, I don't love you anymore, I don't love you anymore*", going over and over in my head as I drove along the motorway.

As I pulled into my own driveway I realised what I would have to do, I would have to tell John, I *had* to.

I didn't love him anymore.

My heart sank into my stomach and bubbled with fear. My hands were like ice and I felt as if I were dangling over a cliff, the hard ground at the bottom ready to obliterate me upon impact.

I'm going in now, I told myself, *with my son asleep in my arms, and I will put him to bed and I will somehow mention to John that I just don't love him.* How was I going to start that conversation? I had no idea, so I put my boy to bed, locked the front door to the house and walked in the kitchen. John was in the living room watching TV, while I poured myself a glass of wine, in a vain attempt to dampen the adrenaline pumping through my body. I really wanted to say it, the words I wanted to say swam around in my mind, but I couldn't find a way to get them out. My heart was about to pop out of my chest when I suddenly heard the TV click off. Silence.

I stared at the kitchen door, and waited to see what he was going to do. I heard his footsteps coming towards the kitchen and there he was in the doorway. The man I had married eighteen years ago, on that rainy March morning, looking at me.

"Are you coming up to bed?" he asked.

A high pitched ringing whistled in my ears.

"No, I am not going to bed with you," I replied. He knew by my face that I had something to say.

"Why not?" he questioned. "Don't you love me anymore?"

Something swelled deep in the pit of my stomach.

"No, I don't love you anymore!" I spat, before I could even register what I was about to say.

I'll never forget that look on his face, he looked at me for a good five seconds with his mouth slack open, whether out of disbelief over what I had said, or over the fact that I had finally verbalised what he probably knew all along, I'm not sure. He started to cry, he sobbed and I just froze, and I stood there, looking at him on the floor. I coldly swept from the room, and heartlessly left him on the floor crying. I padded up the stairs and climbed into my daughter's bed.

The next day I switched off my phone; I'd erased Joey's number and all the messages. I felt so heartless, like some murderous villain, I felt no remorse at all, and I had lost all feeling. I was done with the sorrow. I had felt sorry for him for so many bloody years, I had given up now; I felt nothing for him. No one should ever stay in a relationship due to fear, or feeling sorry for their partner, it's not healthy.

My declaration had made everything worse; neither of us could afford to leave so we were forced to stay together in the same house. I stayed mostly upstairs and he lived downstairs, it was terrible. We lived like this for months and months, I was hardly eating, I didn't even want to eat and my body became hollow and gaunt. I was still trying to lead a relatively normal life, I still had overtime offered at work, and spent quite a lot of time with my family and parents, anything not to be at home. My family knew how it was, but I didn't know what to do next. When we were at home we tried our best to keep the kids happy, but how much longer could this carry on? We both had nowhere to go, and I didn't want the kids to leave their home.

My relationship with Joey grew stronger, I was falling for him hard. It was as though he gave me strength; a push, a reason to finally end my relationship with John, something that should have been done years before, but I never had the bottle to do it. I was feeling strong because I had support from my family and I had my secret relationship to keep me going. Being with Joey made me feel alive, like I had woken up.

We would meet in secret whenever we could, in pubs or a park by my house, it didn't matter, because when I was with Joey I seemed to open up a bit more, come out of myself a bit because I felt happier when I was with him, he was beginning to open up with me too, and we grew closer. In time we both grew to realise that me being married was in the way of us progressing, so I decided that I would tell John I wanted a divorce. I knew I definitely didn't want to spend the next half of my life with him; no way could I carry on in a loveless marriage that was making me feel miserable beyond belief, especially after telling him what I had. I took Joey showing up in my life as a way out, a chance to move on and change my life, which I wanted so desperately.

I was on the lookout for a solicitor to talk to, so I looked on the internet and came across a solicitor in my area that was female and dealt in family law. I booked an appointment; I was scared as hell. My mum came with me, which steadied me a bit, but now I was stepping into the unknown, there was no way of telling where my life would go from here. We waited in the lounge area until I was called in and my stomach lurched, my nerves were shot and my mind clouded with anxiety. As my name was called, I felt like I was about to go on trial, and I prayed that I wouldn't have to go to court with this divorce case. I was anxious to see what she said to the point of feeling physically sick.

Mum and I sat down in the office and we exchanged greetings with the lady.

"I'm here because I want to divorce my husband," I stated.

"On what grounds?" she questioned

"Because I don't love him."

"There has to be something more than that."

"I live upstairs and he lives downstairs in the same house, we've been parted for months, but we both have nowhere to go."

"Who owns the house? And do you work?"

"Both our names are on the deeds, but he pays for it and yeah, I have a part time job. I work officially one day a week."

I was desperate, I never mentioned the man I was having an affair with, and I felt so deceitful, but I pushed that under the carpet and tried my hardest to put it out of my mind.

"He kicked you, didn't he?" mum interjected. I just looked at her and nodded.

"He did, he kicked me in the night and winded me," I concurred. Which was true, it did happen, whether it was deliberate or not, I didn't care. I wished that I hadn't needed to mention it but I was so desperate for a divorce. The lady looked at me.

"We have a case then," she replied, and I sobbed there and then in the solicitor's office.

I didn't care what was going to happen next, all I knew was that I might finally be able to escape, and the relief was so intense that I couldn't help shaking and crying. My mum gave me the biggest warmest hug anyone could ever give, and for a moment I didn't feel so scared.

The divorce proceedings started and John received a letter in the post to ask for a divorce. The atmosphere in the house was terrible; the negative vibes were palpable and I was living on jacket potatoes, which I would take up to my daughter's room to eat. I had moved into her room, she was fifteen at the time, and I was so thin I could fit into her clothes, I looked terrible. If I wanted anything in the kitchen I would wait until I could hear that he was finished before I went down there, and the kids would pass between us.

I wouldn't wish that situation on anyone, it was awkward and upsetting, but when it came down to it, we were both to blame, for our crap attitudes, for my dishonesty and our complete lack of communication.

8 8,991 MILES FROM HOME

Within a few weeks of the divorce papers coming through, my sister broke the news that they had the go ahead to emigrate to Australia.

I didn't want to believe that this was happening, not now, not ever, it was unreal. Selfishly, I was adamant that it would all fall through and hopeful that there might be a glitch somewhere that would stop them. They needed this chance to start a new life in a new environment, but I was only thinking of my loss; the loss of my best friend, my rock, my fun loving sister. *She can't leave me*, especially now I was divorcing, I needed her more than ever, but she was leaving me, and I could do nothing about it.

Even though I had Joey, who my sister still knew nothing about, I couldn't imagine my life without her. She would have been so happy for Joey and I, I knew she would have, but I still never told her in case word got out. I couldn't let that happen while going through the divorce because I had lied and said no one else was involved. I had to keep a roof over my kid's heads, so I lied to survive and save my own skin too. I was scared of having my kids taken away from me and of how bad it'd look if this relationship ever came to light. I was so desperate; a desperate mother would do anything to keep her kids safe.

The news of my sister's move to Australia kept me low for a long time, but I never let on too much that it bothered me, because it was their dream; their goal, and they were happy. How could I intrude on their happiness? So, as their leaving date came closer I kept saying I was happy for them because I knew I still had my parents, my brother and his family, and Joey.

I was drinking at night to drown my sorrows, the numbness felt good and it meant I wouldn't have to think about my sister leaving for a few hours. I would hide the vodka bottles under the bed and tell no one. Every morning would bring a haze of blurred memories and a churning in my gut. At the time I felt I needed it, I couldn't face the nights alone with the thoughts of my sister leaving, or the worry of keeping my relationship a secret, besides, one more drink couldn't hurt, right?

The time came to say goodbye to my special best friend, my sister. They had a big send off party in their local pub in Bethnal Green, just a few doors away from their home. We all said goodbye to them and had a great, drunken night. The time for them to leave came a few weeks later, to leave their home; to leave us. My sister and I made a pact, because we knew how hard this day would be, to have a laugh and joke and say "See you tomorrow!", and really feel like that was going to happen. I tried as hard as I could not to get upset, to train my brain into being totally emotionless, I could not let my emotions get the better of me, it was the hardest day of my life, I felt like I would never see my sister again, but I plucked the thought from my mind.

I could have easily broken down and sobbed at her feet, but we promised each other we'd save the tears. It all happened so quickly. We said goodbye, but I couldn't even look at her, we hugged each other so hard, and we just kept our heads down. When it was all done, I jumped into the car and drove off. The floodgates opened and I sobbed, my knuckles whitening as I gripped the steering wheel. Devastation struck and I wheeled myself onto the side of the road, I was just glad I was able to hold it together in front of her. My baby sister was gone, and depression was sinking in like a cold blade into my chest; I felt myself grieve for her as if she had died.

I just had to keep telling myself I was going to see her tomorrow, but I felt like my heart was ready to explode. I sat there in the car, hot tears rolling down my cheeks; my brain pounding against my skull. I knew I had to get home now and get myself a large vodka, or I wouldn't be able to cope with the waves of sadness crashing against me, I needed it.

I hated that day, my beautiful baby sister, the woman I looked up to more than anyone else had left me. I had written her a letter and made her promise she would only open it when the plane had taken off. The letter told all about Joey, my secret love. It was safe to tell her now. A few weeks later a letter fell onto the porch floor with a dull *plop*, she had written back talking of her excitement, of how ecstatically happy she was for me and wished us well.

I knew I had to keep myself strong for my kids, and totally concentrate on them and the divorce. I knew that Joey had deep feelings for me, which really helped me at the time; it felt like he was sent to me from above at the right time to help me get through the divorce, and the devastation of losing my sister to Australia. He kept me sane; it felt fantastic to be told that I was loved, and I chose to believe that. I was so grateful for him. He was there for me, even though we were a secret. He was my rock at the time and I needed him.

A few months went by and my dad was coming up for retirement, he still worked as a black cab driver in the city and he hated it, retirement couldn't come sooner for him, because my mum had retired years earlier herself. It was okay for a while and although I was hiding my feelings about losing my sister, I coped because of my family and Joey. My parents must have noticed something was up, because I seemed like I was back to normal and happier than before, and they regularly asked me if I was okay. I toyed with the idea of telling them about Joey, I knew it would make them feel better that someone was making me happy, but it would have to wait a while longer.

As usual, the kids and I, as well as my brother, his wife and kids were all visiting my parents.

"We're glad you're all here because we want to ask you something," my mum chimed. We waited eagerly, the moment pregnant with anticipation. "Me and Daddy are thinking of selling up and moving to Spain. What do you think?"

My heart sank again. I knew my dad had had enough of the UK, he was always complaining about the British government, how much they ripped us all off and how they wouldn't survive properly as pensioners here. Yet I felt as if someone had grabbed my heart and squeezed until it popped. I had Joey, and what with my sister leaving I had learned to be stronger, so I wished them well, and held back the tears. There was no way I could have stopped them for my own selfish reasons, and even if I wanted to I knew I wouldn't have found the words to change their minds.

Besides, I reasoned, *Spain isn't that far away, only two hours on a plane.* I was trying again to hide my real feelings; and years of practise had made me surprisingly good at it. I wanted the best for them, the very best for my very loving parents, even though it was devastating to think of how my family were all gradually leaving me to explore the world, and I was being left alone again.

I was going through a divorce, my sister had gone and now my parents were going to leave as well. What next? My brother? My kids? *Please don't take anybody else away*, I would think. I clung to my kids and Joey for dear life after that. I lied through my teeth to the solicitor and to John about the affair. I couldn't have my babies taken away from me.

In the space of a year, my life had gone from bad to catastrophically disastrous. Somehow I carried on, I even managed to pretend I was happy even though sometimes I honestly wanted to die. I would say the drinking kept me happier at the time, when I was alone, but it didn't. It only numbed and dulled my mind to a state of emptiness that I had confused for happiness. Perhaps it had been so long since I'd felt truly happy that I'd forgotten what it even felt like. I could enter a place of blissful ignorance of the world, until the hangover kicked me in the face the next day. Sometimes when I woke up, groggy and hungover, it felt like it was all a dream; that none of what had happened was real. I would drink at night when the kids were settled and they were safe indoors with John and I. I just slaughtered myself because it was numbing my brain and my thoughts. I was still smoking heavily as well; I looked and felt like shit. I was getting thinner by the day, but Joey was the string that kept me from falling over the edge.

I went to visit my parents one evening, my dad was out and I had plucked up the courage to tell my mum about Joey. I told her I had met a bloke at work and he had been a secret for quite a while, I told her everything. I got upset while telling the story of my secret life-saver because I knew it was wrong and she cried with me. Tears of sadness and tears of happiness, because now she could move to Spain knowing I had someone to look after me, to help me and support me. We hugged and the relief was overwhelming. She asked when she could meet him, and I laughed. She was serious, so we arranged a date and I invited Joey to meet my parents. This was the test, would he want to meet them, was he that serious about me?

Joey was over the moon; he couldn't wait to meet them, this felt so right. They got along like a house on fire; we all had a great night and a real laugh. Joey and my dad really hit it off because Joey was so funny, and I couldn't stop beaming. They liked him even though he was a lot younger than me, even though he didn't seem it. Mum said we suited each other well.

The day came for my parents to leave, and it seemed as if time had passed in the blink of an eye since they'd told us. Another devastating day; the feelings from the day my sister left came rushing back to me. Again, I found myself trying my hardest to stay composed, to not show my hurt, mum and I wanted it like this.

"See you next week," I gulped back the tears.

"See you soon," they replied.

Fake, happy goodbyes were exchanged again. My parents reassured me that if they didn't like it they would soon come back. To hear that made it a bit easier, but still, my mum and dad were leaving me. I was alone again; another piece of my family was gone.

I had to be hard at the airport, it was all so bloody fake and it made it even harder to say goodbye. Would I ever even see my parents again?

Why was all of this happening to me? I knew life changed, but not this much, and not all at once. It's so strange how life pans out; we know nothing of our futures or how our life journeys are going to go. At the time I knew less about my future than most, I still had no goals or future dreams, divorce papers and secrecy were all I saw ahead of me; all I knew was that I wanted to be happy again. I wanted Joey in my life, my God send, my rock. I was clinging to him for dear life now more than ever, I had no one else, and I was needing him more and more.

9 EIGHT DOORS AWAY

I agreed that when my son was eighteen years old I would give John 15% of what the house was worth at the time, and that he would give the children £30 a week until they were 18. I couldn't be bothered to fight him or ask for more money for the kids, to dispute the house or disagree in any way because I wanted it all to end, a quick, clean separation.

My solicitor told me that if I did more hours in the supermarket I could take over the mortgage, get a loan to pay John off now and give the rest when my son turned eighteen. So that's what I did. It made the mortgage monthly payments higher, but I was on low income so I qualified for tax credit; to say I was scraping the bottom of the barrel would be a gross understatement.

Of course, my now ex-husband had to buy another home, however, I'm not sure I could accurately put into words how I felt when I discovered he had bought a house on the same street as me, eight doors away; easily viewable every time I left the house, but I'll try.

At first, I was in disbelief, that the man that I had waited years to get away from had actually bought a home opposite me. I couldn't believe it was happening; neither could the solicitor, my friends or family. I knew he hated my guts because of what I'd done to him; to our family, I had taken his home from him and I knew he suspected I was having an affair. He had every right to hate me, so would he not have been happier to never set eyes on me again?

He can see my every move, I thought, *he just wants to spoil my life even more.*

Apparently, it was to be closer to his children because he feared losing them, which I would never have allowed to happen. He was their dad and he always would be. We agreed that I would have the children in the week and he would have them at weekends and a Monday, so we were equal.

The day came when he had to move out; we had been living in the same house for over a year, yet completely separated, I couldn't wait to finally be free. It was a Sunday, I had been at work all day and I came home that evening, turned the key in the door and pushed it open.

It was empty, everything had gone; he'd left nothing but the dust on the floor. I had said in the consent order that he could take everything in the house other than one sofa, the oven and the kid's beds. He'd taken the rest.

I slid to the floor and cried my heart out. Tears of relief dampened my cheeks, relief and joy and disbelief that finally I was free.

That sweet moment of freedom, however, was fleeting. I still saw him nearly every day, it was hard to even step outside and not automatically look left to see if he was there. The man I had been married to for so long, we had a history together, children together, good and bad times together. The man I'd tried so hard to get rid of was still in my life. It wasn't right but neither was what I'd done. I'd dealt with the situation all wrong, I'd been dishonest and sneaky and now karma was coming back for me. My friends and family would tell me how wrong it was for him to decide to live so close to me, how they found it hard to understand, but they didn't know the full truth. They asked how the kids felt about it, well, my son was only eleven and it didn't seem to bother him, in fact he was quite excited that he had two bedrooms and two lots of toys and two gardens, plus two Christmases and two birthdays, he was fine. He was always an easy going; happy child, so I tried to make it sound fun and positive for him. My daughter, on the other hand, was older and it hit her hard. Fifteen is not a good age for your parents to split up; I sometimes wished that it all happened earlier in the kids' lives so they wouldn't have fully understood and it wouldn't have affected them as much.

My daughter had many issues going on in her life, not only had her cousin and best friend emigrated to Australia, but her boyfriend and I argued incessantly. All I would ever hear was my daughter on the phone to him, they would be arguing and I felt that he was always upsetting my girl. One night, while in the middle of another argument, I grabbed the phone from her and told him to stop upsetting my daughter and never come around here ever again. I had enough going on at the time, and this was the only way I could handle it. We were all arguing constantly and the atmosphere in our home was terrible. The negative vibes were powerful, which created even more negativity, because like attracts like. Thankfully, our heated relationship didn't last long, thanks to family members helping to mend things, but it taught me a valuable lesson about when to just let old anger go and move on with your life.

I look back now and admit that at the time I couldn't see the way my choices were affecting my daughter. She was obviously very down and low herself; she would have regular panic attacks, which prompted me to arrange for her to have counselling.

Divorce is a terrible trauma in life and it affects everyone, it's sad, but it happens so often. People change, circumstances change and lack of communication played a big part in the downfall of my own marriage. I tried my best the best way I knew how at the time, and I'm eternally sorry for putting my children through that. No child deserves to see their parent's hatred for one another, and as a mother I know that saying sorry is never good enough, but I now have even more love to show them than ever before.

The divorce papers finally came through; the whole world must have heard my cries of relief that day; felt my tears of overwhelming joy. Not many people could ever imagine the feelings of the mixed emotions I felt that day. It was the end of an era, a total change of life for me. A new direction; I was now fully independent, I could finally breath. I cried on and off all day, in between texting and calling everyone I knew, including Joey.

I was so happy, Joey and I could talk freely in my home now, I could set off and drive to his nan's house at weekends and not feel guilty. I didn't care that he had nothing, hardly any money, no independence and no prospects. All I knew was that I was free and in love. Everything was rock and roll; I was alive, I was living and loving, and it felt fantastic.

A few months passed and my parents came home to visit from Spain, I remember my mum asking me when I was going to tell the kids. In truth I was a bit nervous about it.

"You'll have to tell them sooner or later," she'd remark.

I was dreading what they would say, especially my daughter, as she was older and would notice the age difference. Would they accept us or not?

"Mummy has a new friend," I said to my kids one night. My heart was pounding; I was cringing inside as I said it, waiting for them to react.

They both raised their eyebrows; I told them his name and I explained what he looked like and the interests we shared, like our music taste, because my son was a budding rock star and was into metal music too, at the time.

"He has lots of tattoos and he's extremely funny." I couldn't praise him enough, though I left the part about him being younger than me for the end.

"What do you think, kids?"

"Cool," my son smiled. "He sounds good, mum."

My daughter just smiled and gave a succinct "Okay mum."

They were brilliant. What a relief. This was getting better and better, I felt so happy about it all. That my kids might accept my new boyfriend was all I wanted to hear.

I couldn't wait to tell Joey, we were ecstatic; it was all falling into place so perfectly. It was what we wanted and everything was almost too good to be true. I had lost almost everything in my life and yet, my life seemed to be getting better, my happiness was radiating out there into the Universe, and we were attracting more happiness back to us, unaware at the time that the Law of Attraction was doing what it does.

In my head I was telling myself, convincing myself that the sixteen year age gap didn't matter, that it would all be okay. I was young at heart and he was older in the head, it would all even itself out.

I wasn't seeing any of my old friends, we all just kind of drifted apart; we had our own lives to lead. We were close at one point and we would get together and have a few bottles of wine or go out but now it was different. I suppose it was my doing, I never contacted them; we all had our issues going on at that time anyway. One of our friends was very ill, another had lost one of her parents and I was divorcing, we all went through big trauma at the time, and it all changed. I was a bit scared to tell them of my new found love who was so many years younger than me. I was scared of what they would say and if they would ask too many questions so I stayed away from them. I *did* care about what people thought of me. I had one friend who was special to me, she started as a distant friend, a girl I knew at the school gate while picking up our kids. We became closer because she didn't judge me and was very easy going. She was my drinking partner; we had some great nights drinking. We would meet at her home once a week and look forward to trying out different drink combinations and listening to our mad music and laughing so much, it was fantastic. As usual, the next day would be a succession of rolling headaches and dehydration.

I was so excited about seeing Joey at the weekends; I tried my hardest not to let him know I was a drinker. I did drink in front of him, but I managed to kerb it, like it wasn't a problem. It felt like going cold turkey at times, so I would pig out on junk food instead, and on Sunday evenings at home I would look forward to a large vodka or nice bottle of wine.

Friday nights couldn't come around quick enough, I could see and hold someone who loved me, which he told me so sixteen times a day and I did the same, whether through a text or a phone call, it felt so great. He showed his loving ways, which made me fall harder every time. I was besotted and I felt so lucky for the first time in a long time. I tried my hardest to keep a young outlook, you're as young as you feel, or as young as the man you're feeling more like. I'd say I was okay with our age gap, even though sometimes it bothered me, but I never said; I just kept my feelings in again. As young as Joey made me feel, the woman who stared back at me from within the mirror, whose forehead lines ran deep across her face, was not the woman I knew myself to be inside.

We made life plans that we never achieved because we had no drive or no money, I was barely getting by and he was in and out of jobs like a yoyo. I decided I wanted to be more positive in my life, so I started to look for some positive thinking books online, I didn't know what I was looking for as I had only ever read magazines or newspapers now and then, until I came across a book called "*Love Life, Live Life.*", by a lady called Sue Stone. Sue's picture was displayed on the cover; her face instantly reminded me of two of the people I missed most, my mum and sister. She had bright blonde hair, a lovely tan and a nice smile just like them, and before I knew it I had ordered myself a copy.

The book came and I was eager to take a look at it, I had never read an entire book in my life, I would always start to read but never follow it through, because I was lazy minded. I read it when I could, but only bits of it would sink in, alcohol had obliterated my memory and I would soon forget what I'd read, so I put it down, besides, I was more interested in sex, junk food and alcohol all weekend.

I had a hobby, painting furniture, which I didn't really take that seriously. I doubted myself and my abilities; I told myself that I was a bit crap at it and it was only paint, even though people told me otherwise. I had the training, I knew what undercoats to use on what surfaces and what effects and colours would go best, I could make a piece of old brown wood look like a beautiful, cream, shabby chic piece of art, which would sell in Kensington for hundreds if you slapped a designer label on it. The more people were telling me this, the more I was thinking of how I could earn something substantial out of it. So I designed a leaflet and got a few hundred printed up from a friend, and I half heartedly went out posting through people's letterboxes in the posh areas. I was scared because I was thinking the worst, of all the bad scenarios that could come from this, but trying to remember some of the stuff in Sue's book too.

I was pushing myself, coming out of my comfort zone. I feared any work coming in, and nothing happened for a few weeks, until I started to really visualise how great it would be if I could make a business out of it. Not having to get up at stupid o'clock to be in the supermarket and slog for a company that thinks nothing of me. I would love to run a business, and it was on my mind quite a bit. A few more weeks and I went out happily posting again; I gave out hundreds of flyers and I never gave up until they were all gone. I got home and I had a phone call, my very first phone call from a lady I had never met, who wanted to see pictures of what I was capable of. I couldn't believe it, my first potential client! She hired me, and I did a brilliant job, it was only a small cabinet but it got the ball rolling. It was the start of something good.

So I was a single mum, with a part time job I also had working and child tax credit, and I was barely getting by. I had the odd paint job here and there which was my pocket money, it wasn't much, things were tight and I had a mortgage and lots of bills which made everything even more confusing. I always worried about how I was going to get by; the feeling of panic was ever present at the back of my mind. I wasn't about to ask Joey to move in with me, because I knew I would lose the tax credit if we went legal and he wasn't stable enough with work. I had to be sensible, and put me and my kids first, no matter how much I loved him.

10 IT'S ONLY A RING

About a year or so later, Joey told me we were all going out for a meal with his family that had been booked at an Indian restaurant. There were about ten of us, and we had a good time. At the end of the meal I went off to the ladies, when I returned to my seat; Joey was sitting opposite me, and he held my hands across the table, smiling at me. He produced a little box and slid it across the table to me. I looked down at it.

"What's this?" I asked.

"Open it," he prompted, so I did, and there, twinkling up at me was a ring, an engagement ring. I looked at him in amazement.

"Would you do me the honour of being my wife?"

You could have smacked me in the face with a lamp post, I was absolutely stunned, with my mouth open I looked down the table to see everybody looking at me in anticipation, all smiling at me wide eyed, waiting for my answer.

I certainly did not expect that. I really loved him, more than I could ever express, but I had no intention of getting married again whatsoever. After all those years married to John, another marriage was the last thing on my mind. It had not been that long ago that I had divorced. Why did he want this?

I had to answer, they were all looking at me. *It's only a ring,* I thought, *it's only a ring, it's not set in stone, I can change my mind.* I looked at him, and to save any upset, I said yes, but I felt more awkward than anything else.

I knew there was no way I was going to upset this man and his whole family. *I won't take it as a promise, besides, people stay engaged for years.* I must have known in my heart that something was stopping me. I was happy to have and accept his ring, but marriage still scared me.

The difference was, I didn't really love my first husband how I should have, but I really loved Joey. It was his instability with his work and our ages that stopped me from giving myself completely.

A few years passed and we got more content, the time went so quickly; we both put on weight, and I began to look a bit older. I certainly felt older and very unfit, and when I put on weight it all settles around my middle, my tummy and waistline. I didn't feel all that good about myself, but Joey's belly was even bigger and the weight showed in his face as well. I remember thinking to myself *if he carries on the way he's going he'll probably die of a heart attack.* He smoked heavily as well, and if he looked like this now, what would he look like when he was in his forties? I worried about his health; both of our lifestyles were unhealthy at the time. We consumed a hell of a lot of McDonalds, KFC, pizza, anything we could get our hands on, and Joey had a vicious sweet tooth; he could eat chocolate on tap without feeling sick. I was getting to look the same, I had put on about two stone since we met, and the sly drinking on the side wasn't helping either. I'm sure he could see that I was gradually opening up with the drinking habit I had, we would lounge around most of the time we spent together, watching horror films or silly American comedies, a lot of our weekends were being wasted on TV and junk food and doing not much at all, but he was funny and he made me laugh like no one else. I thought I needed him, his charming words. I was addicted to him, and the TV and the junk food. He had become a familiar fixture in my world.

Soon, things started to change, even though he didn't live with me I found myself trying to give him advice about the way he spent, or should I say squandered, his money. I had loads to pay out, what with all the bills and mortgage and food shopping; I never had much spare but I did make sure I had a couple hundred put away just in case. I was trying to be independent, but a bit of help from Joey now and then would have been nice. I didn't ask; I never would. When he was out of work both me and his family would help him, even though I was the one with all the bills and a home to run. I tried to advise him about stuff and sometimes I felt like I was his mum. It would all come flooding back to me, that's what John had done to me, tried to make me understand about the cost of living while I would shrug him off. I didn't want to hear it, and I had taken my ex for granted big time. Now I felt Joey doing it to me, was this how John had felt when he spoke to me? This felt like the beginning of my Karma.

Joey would waste his money when he had it, I couldn't figure out what he was buying all the time, as most of his expenses were covered at his nan's flat. He was always in the red with his bank, which was pretty unnerving for me considering that I was engaged to him.

Waking up one Monday morning, I'd had a drink the night before and I was feeling as rough as anything; feeling like absolute crap and sad that I wouldn't see Joey for another five days unless he popped by mid week. I heard the door bell go off; I padded downstairs, greeted the postman and noticed I had a package from Australia. I was eager to open it because I knew it would be from my sister. I tried to feel excited but I felt miserable, not even this was going to bring me out of the dumps, apparently. In the package was a DVD. I didn't take that much notice of it, and tucked it away in my bedroom drawer for when I was feeling in the mood to watch it.

Because I really fancied Joey, and I didn't get to see him all week, I was extremely sex orientated; it was always on my mind because I missed him. He told me I was driving him mad wanting sex all the time, he would spend more and more time on the phone at the weekend to his friends or his mum, or he'd want to watch TV or play videogames, which I hated. We only had the weekend together, and I worked all day Sundays, so we didn't have that much time together in my eyes, and because he was broad and chunky and charming, I fancied the pants off of him and I wanted more sex. I had given up smoking and I could breathe a bit better, so I had the energy and stamina. I would give hints at first, like taking a shower and smelling good and wearing something sexy and over exaggerated, trying my hardest, and sometimes he just didn't want to know. It never used to be like this, I didn't understand, *I'm not that disgusting am I?*

"It's not all about sex all the time, you know," he would say, which I know now but back then I had the urge and I fancied him and I loved him, so I wanted to share myself with him. Instead I ended up feeling rejected, I thought he must be going off of me, and then I'd drive myself mad with all the thoughts whirling around in my head, about how I was getting old, how I looked crap. I would tell myself *I know he will cheat on me, I know he will* and then I'd upset myself by imagining him with someone else, cheating on me, just as I cheated on my husband.

Looking back his phone was on 24/7 and he was continually on it. I wanted him to myself, I only saw him Friday nights, Saturday all day and Sunday evening after I got home from work. I loved his company, but when the days were wasted on the phone to all sorts of friends and family, I tried to be cool but inside I was screaming, "*What about me! What about me!*" I got told I was loved ten times a day, but it was only words, words that cover things up or shut you up. It kept me sweet, and I would give in and forgive him because he had an angelic face, and a charm about him.

He still rang me numerous times a day in the week; almost too many times at one point, "I love you" being thrown back and forth, numerous times in one conversation. I knew he loved me because I hadn't had it in my first marriage.

I had attracted this person to me, I had asked for a lover who was opposite to my ex husband, little did I know that the opposite of my ex husband was me. Joey's easy going nature had begun to come across as lazy, with a 'can't be bothered' attitude, promises of the world but no action. Is this how I had been all those years ago? The universe seemed to be holding up a mirror of all my faults and pushing my face up against the glass.

My Karma was hitting harder than ever; sometimes I would catch myself sounding and acting just like John to make Joey see the light, to turn him into the person I wanted him to be. The only friends we would ever see were Joey's mates, mostly single young men who had no girlfriends because they preferred racing around in their cars at night. I introduced Joey to my neighbours a few doors away because they were similar to us, with Jane being older than her husband Tom, I thought Joey and Tom would get along well, and give us some more adult company than his other friends. They got on great, and they often smoked themselves silly outside my front door at the weekends, chatting about cars and music.

On most Saturday nights, when I went to bed for my 5am start, Joey would hang out with Tom on my drive. A few more of his friends would turn up and I could hear them all outside laughing while I was trying to sleep, much to my complete and utter annoyance. I could have exploded and shouted from the window, but then I'd become even more like John, the way he acted that night when he kicked me, so I just let it be.

I told him one day that it was keeping me awake, so he started to go out on a Saturday night while I was in bed for work the next day. He told me he was going racing on the motorways, and that they would all park up and admire one another's cars. What?! This was just too teenage for me, why hadn't I seen this coming? He was in his twenties, and I was gradually getting more and more pissed off with the whole situation, but I loved him like mad so I accepted it and just got on with it. Inside I began to feel bad that I could never give this man any children, being sterilised when my youngest was six years old, and I would not adopt, I started to think of what future we had together, if any. It's funny, how when everything is going well and it's all new and exciting, you can see a brilliant bright future; when you feel bad and it's going tits up or not how you planned then you begin to question the future and ask, "Do I really want this? How can I change it?" All the scenarios whizz around your head, you over-analyse everything and drive yourself mad assuming things. But my fear of being alone outweighed all of this.

I had been through a divorce and turned my whole world upside down for this life I have now, and I have to make the best of it. My kids were precious to me and I know Joey loved children; it was on my mind a lot that I couldn't give him kids, we talked about this from the start of our relationship, and he said it didn't bother him. I was telling myself more and more that he could be cheating on me when he was out; my insecurities were rotting my mind and turning my brain to mush.

I always told him we could be completely honest with each other and talk things through, *let's not have any secrets*, and we agreed. I asked that if he ever did cheat or meet anyone to tell me and save me the embarrassment of finding out myself, and he agreed. He always called me babe, and I felt loved.

11 RED FLAGS

One of my birthdays was coming up, although I don't remember which, they all seem to blur into one the older you get and the more alcohol you drink, what I can remember is that I didn't want it to come, because I was getting older. My birthday is in January, which is a month of financial crisis for most people, so I've never had expensive birthday gifts but I was fine with that.

Joey asked me what I wanted for my birthday, and I assumed, as always, that he didn't have much money, but a little gift would be nice. He was a generous natured person if he had money, and he had good intentions. I chose a cheap dress ring from Argos that I liked and we drove in my van to have a look at it. When we got there he passed me a wad of folded notes.

"You go in and get it." I had to go in and get my own birthday gift; he didn't offer to come in with me. It upset me that he couldn't even be bothered, but I just shut up and got it myself, because I knew I probably wouldn't get anything otherwise.

In September 2010 we were sat watching TV as usual at my house, when I asked to look at his phone. Up until then I had 100% access to it and we would often swap each other's phones and mess about on them, but this time it was different.

"Why?" He asked, as he held it to himself to show me what I wanted to see, panic seemed to flash across his face, it made me feel uneasy. I passed him the phone back in case I found something I didn't want to see, ignorance is bliss as they say.

Weeks before this, over the weekend, I noticed some new friends of his and Tom's hanging around outside my door on a Saturday night, all young men with their girlfriends in tow. One of the girls had a loud mouth and flirty attitude to match, and she was all over her boyfriend like a rash. I could hear her swearing and being rude, and they would all be laughing at her antics. I managed to catch a glimpse of her through the bedroom window; she was tiny and slim and tanned, with long dark hair.

I noticed Joey's behaviour when they were chatting, he was acting flirty and she seemed to focus on him. *But he's flirty anyway*, I told myself, *whether he knows he's doing it or not*. I don't know why, but I knew he liked her; she kept checking her reflection in my van mirror; I could see Joey looking at her and my instinct kicked me harder.

I never saw him the next day because he had the worst hangover. All week I had had nightmares of him being unfaithful to me. He came over the following Friday and he seemed different, a bit distant; not so happy to see me, out of character and secretive. Still taking calls on his phone, but something felt wrong, I sensed it but I couldn't pin point it. I watched him closely; making mental notes to myself, there was just something I didn't trust. I watched his every move all weekend, like John must have done to me when he thought I was cheating on him. I didn't give Joey a chance, I just assumed, he seemed unhappy a lot more often but I never confronted him, he just wasn't the man I knew, or thought I knew. The bad dreams continued, and I was waking up in the night in a cold sweat, the word karma going around and around in my head.

In my nightmares I was shouting at cold dark hissing dragons as big as Dinosaurs in a dingy, grey dungeon.

"I know this is my karma! I know this is my payback!" I would scream at them. They would just coldly stare at me through emotionless, black eyes.

I knew from then on that I had to end this, the dreams were a sign, a big, flashing red warning sign. Stand up and say something, be brave, end it.

He wasn't right for me, even though I loved him, being with him sent negative thoughts through my mind, it drove me to madness. Everything I could see in him was negative, his ways, his laziness, his empty words and his junky habits, his nonexistent promises, his videogame and TV addiction, his low libido, all his bad habits, his heavy smoking, his lack of commitment to study the plumbing course he was supposed to be on, his lack of ambition, his friends who he put first and his precious car that I had bought him, his secretive ways. He was just pulling the wool over my stupid eyes, and I needed to confront him, he didn't love me, he was just using me. I felt I was standing under a big, dark cloud and it was raining freezing cold black rain on me. I needed to break free again, I had to be hard and strong, to stop pussy footing around and get a hold on myself.

This was 100% Karma, because this is exactly how I was with John. The old me was living in my boyfriend, giving me a dose of my own medicine, it had come back around and bit me in the arse. What goes around, comes around and that was the biggest lesson in my life that I have ever learned. NEVER underestimate Karma, because it definitely gets you. It has made me realise to only treat people with respect, ask for what you want, and treat others as you would like to be treated.

But back then, I had a plan, I got up into my loft and collected all of Joey's boxes, all the stuff that he had stored up there, all his clutter and junk that had been at his nan's and his mum's places. It took me days to get it all down into the living room; I rang him and asked if he was coming over, he was out late the night before and was too tired to come, so I made an excuse.

"Please, my van has broken down, I need you." I got upset on the phone, so he drove over to me. I had already loaded all his stuff into the back of my van so he could just transfer it to his car.

He walked abruptly in through my front door, and he looked tired and unhappy. I was standing on my stairs in the living room, opposite my front door.

"What's up with the van?" He asked.

My heart was racing, it was thumping out of my chest, I couldn't believe I was about to do this again.

"Joey, I have something to say." I looked into his crystal blue eyes, they were the palest, ice blue ever, even though he was tired, he still looked handsome and broad, the sun was shining on his face and he had a tuft of blonde on his chin. I could see his beauty again, he looked like an angel in the sun, just looking at me, waiting for me to say something, and I gulped. This was going to be the hardest thing I had ever done.

"I think we should split up." The words escaped my lips before I even realised what I'd said, and I held my hand over my mouth, as if I'd be able to catch the sentence before it reached his ears. I don't know what I expected, but he went ballistic.

"WHAT?!"

I took off my engagement ring to give it back to him.

"I just don't trust you anymore; I think you're cheating on me." I had to force the words out.

He swore and ranted and raved and denied it.

"I don't trust you," I said again, hot tears rolling down my cheeks. "I need my life back!" I shouted. I explained it all to him, but I could barely get my words out through the sobbing. It hurt, more than I had ever been hurt before, I was letting go of something I loved. It was so hard, but it was my choice, it was what I wanted.

After about an hour of crying and talking, with me explaining what he didn't do for our relationship, I told him that I really wanted him to go and live properly with someone his own age, someone who could give him children.

"Please, I need to be alone. I needed space." My trust for him had been obliterated by my own mind. "It'll never be the same."

We cuddled so hard in each other's arms, and sobbed for what seemed like an age, but I was not going to change my mind. He finally said he understood; it was all so emotional. I don't know why I didn't get angry, I could have ranted and raged about it but I wanted peace, I wanted a peaceful end. I was sick of all the worrying and the assuming because he totally denied most of it, he had admitted that there were girls he was interested in, but I knew in my heart that he was unfaithful to me. That he was telling me lies, and he was using me for my home comforts to get away from his little room in his nan's flat. It wasn't until it was all over that my daughter said to me that she could see right through him, she could see he was using me, and some of my neighbours said the same to me too.

So he left, we unpacked the van and transferred all his stuff into his car, hugged again and said our goodbyes, in tears, of course. He drove away and I watched him go.

I walked indoors and I sobbed like a baby, my head felt like it had split in two from all the crying, and it was killing me. I cried on and off for the next five hours, just moping about the house, the kids were at their dad's so I was free to wallow in my misery. My neighbours must have heard me crying through the walls.

My phone rang; Joey's name flashed up on the screen. I didn't answer; I couldn't, even though I was tempted. He left a voice mail. I should have erased it, but I listened. He just said my name and I could hear him crying. My heart melted, and all the good times we had came flooding back to me. I stupidly rang him back.

I just wanted to say sorry to him once more, but I melted, I gave in, again. *Why am I such a mug?* I thought.

We arranged to meet, and he came over to me the next day. We met at my front door and we laughed at the state of our faces, our fat, puffy eyes and red noses from all the sobbing. We laughed as we hugged tightly on my front step, and I felt some relief that I was with him again. We sat in my kitchen with some tea, and we held hands over the table, just then my daughter came in and saw us.

"Babe," I said to her, "me and Joey broke up yesterday but we're going to try again." She just looked at us before heading back over to her dad's house for dinner. She told me after that that I was a mug for going back with him, and I tried to explain myself away, convincing myself it was ok.

As we were sitting at my table telling each other how terrible we had both acted yesterday, he came out with it.

"I was so upset, Kim, I thought to myself, we're not going to live in our big house in Brentwood, and have a skateboard park built on our massive acres of land."

It all came rushing back to me, that was a fun plan we had made together at the very beginning of our relationship, and we would have a good laugh about it. But I had changed and grown up now. I was in my forties and the image of grungy parties with all his mates and their young grungy girlfriends, in my home, like an MTV Rock video sickened me.

That image stuck in my head. He was still using me for my home then and his easy safe secure ready-made future, he was in and out of jobs like a yoyo and couldn't even stick to a plumbing course. So we had some more tea, and he went home and left me to my thoughts. I was so confused, the bad dreams continued, and I was getting angry at myself for calling him back on the day I ended it.

After that my brain began to scramble, I felt like I was going mad. I began talking to myself a lot to ease the mental torture this relationship was putting me through. I didn't want him but I couldn't live without him. I knew he was no good for me but I needed him. My brain wanted to explode, *what do I do?* I was getting signs a lot, more stuff coming to me again on TV and through the radio and adverts. I would overhear conversations all about breaking up, divorce and relationship problems, it was weird and unbelievable. I honestly thought I was losing my marbles.

I was sad and low, probably the lowest I had been so far. I couldn't even cry now, I'd reached a place beyond tears, beyond mere sadness. I had had just about enough, Joey had left all his boxes and junk, they stood in piles in my living room, always in the way whenever I tried to move around. I felt a rage wash over me, unlike any anger I'd ever felt before. I threw them all back in the van, save for a few bags of clothes and CDs. That was it; I've got to tell him, it's over for good.

I was still adamant that he was carrying on with someone else. I had to go to his flat, I hadn't eaten properly for weeks and I was tired, sick and angry. My cheeks had become sunken and my skin sickly and pale. In my rage I ripped open the black bags, smashing up all the CDs and scattering his clothes across the floor. I ran into the kitchen, grabbing bottles of bleach and ketchup and anything else that would leave a mark, and I poured bleach and food onto his clothes; I wrote swear words all over his tee shirts in permanent marker, and a couple of cans of tinned food went in too. I screwed it all up into a soggy, foul smelling ball and stuffed it all into the bags. I bit my tongue in an effort to calm my rage, but I would have hit anyone who crossed my path then.

I jumped into my van, all his ruined belongings thrown in the back, and started toward his place. Driving up the motorway towards his house the traffic was busy, but it was flowing, my knuckles were white from gripping the wheel so hard. I pulled up at his nan's flats, leaving all the boxes in the van but I went up the two flights of stairs with the black bags full of sodden, bleached clothing in tow. I knocked even though I knew he wouldn't be home from work until six. His nan answered, I tried to behave as normal as possible and she let me in. She tottered off to the living room and I dumped the bags in his room, my heart pounding so hard against my chest I thought it might break a rib. I didn't know what I was going to say or do, so I waited in the living room with his nan and we watched TV.

At six, I heard the key in the door, he went straight in his room, and I could hear he was on the phone to someone. He spoke in a low mumble and I knew this was the other woman I thought he had been seeing. My heart felt like it was going to come out of my mouth, adrenalin was coursing through my veins; I could barely stop my hands from shaking. I heard him rustling through the bags.

"WHAT THE FUCK IS ALL THIS?!" he bellowed down the hall.

I jumped up and went storming into the room. I was shouting and screaming and accusing him, all the built up anger came spilling out. We were shouting in each other's faces and I was pushing his chest so hard, hoping to start a fight, but he didn't move. I went ballistic at him while he sat on his bed and I shouted "I know you're seeing her, I heard you on the phone!" He denied it, he looked angry as if he could have easily knocked me out, but he just sat down and kept shouting at me, telling me that I was mad. His Nan came up to see what was going on and he took her into the other room. I glimpsed my house keys on his side cabinet, they were on his car keys, and I just grabbed the lot and I ran. I ran out of the flat and bounded down the stairs as fast as I could in a blind panic; I heard him slam the door behind me. I was too scared to go back, realising that I'd taken all of his keys; my feet didn't touch the ground until I got to the van, jumped in and drove off.

Back up the motorway toward home. I had totally lost the plot; I drove along sobbing to myself, telling myself that he was going to kill me. I had his car keys and he was going to kill me. I could imagine him killing me in my head, so I phoned the police, screaming down the phone at them. "He's going to kill me! I've got his keys!" They took my address and told me to calm down, I had never had a panic attack like that before in my life, it was pure agony.

I had twenty-seven missed calls from him on my phone by the time I got home but I was too scared to answer them. My brain was scrambled, I hadn't meant to take his car keys, I just saw my keys and ran. All the drama and the hate and rage ate away at me and I couldn't control myself. Our brain is so powerful, what goes over and over in our minds, eventually gets accepted as a belief, it becomes reality and our truth, and it can drive us mad.

I hid in the loft thinking he wouldn't think to look for me there. I had terrible visions in my head of all the ways he could hurt me. Realising he had no way to get here without his car keys, I sat up there for a while and tried to calm down. The loft was pitch black and freezing cold; damp leaked in from outside and all I could do was bring my knees to my chest and try to keep warm. When I had calmed down a bit I went back downstairs to find the police were at my door. I let them in, my face red and puffy from crying, and they began to question me. I was stuttering from the cold and could barely string a sentence together. I heard one of the officers radio in and confirm that the incident was just a domestic. The door bell rang and panic rose up in my throat again, I wanted to run and lock myself in the loft again and never come down. An officer went out and after a while came back in.

"He only wants his keys, can he go please?" I handed over the keys and another officer continued the questioning. I just wanted to lock myself away and get my head together.

KIM WYMER

12 …AND I NEVER SAW HIM AGAIN

A few days passed and I heard nothing from him. Panic and anxiety began to frequent me less and less, even though visions of him still swam in the back of my mind. After a week my parents rang from Spain, announcing that they were coming home to visit me. I missed them so much, and needed them here more than ever, but how could I say that to them? They were having the time of their lives and I didn't want to upset or worry them. I suppose I had always taken them for granted, but it's not until you get older and things happen in life that you realise that love is everything.

My parents came home and it was so exciting. I picked them up at the airport and we were like teenagers, laughing and being silly, they completely picked me up and lifted me out of the anger and anxiety that had clouded my mind the past weeks.

My phone buzzed at the table, I'd received a text from Joey. My dad was standing with me as I read his name on my phone. I looked at him, I had told my parents every excruciating detail of what had happened between Joey and I, and he just gave me a discerning look. It had been a few weeks now and I was feeling a bit stronger. I was ready to see what he had to say.

"*Can I ring you? Just to talk, and say a proper goodbye.*" So I agreed.

He rang and we were on the phone for a while, he wanted to meet up to say goodbye for real, so I agreed. We arranged to meet at a park we used to meet at secretly, not too far away from my house. Dad asked if I wanted him to come along, but my gut feeling told me it was going to be calm and okay. I just trusted my instinct, besides I wanted to part on good terms. I wanted peace. I told dad where the park was, though, just in case.

I was stronger and I was not going to take any shit or sweet talk. I drove to the park, we met in the café and he bought me a coffee. We talked for hours, trying to weed through every hitch and bump along the road of our relationship and, eventually, sorted it all out. We both asked our questions, but he still denied cheating on me. I had no real hard proof, not that it mattered now anyway. We both knew and agreed that we had expired and our relationship had run its course, we both wanted different things now, we knew we had learned from each other.

It was a lovely sunny day, even though it was a cold November afternoon. Not another person in sight; the park stood around us in complete, crystalline peacefulness, the morning dew drops still clung to the grass and glittered in the dazzling sun. We said our goodbyes, hugging so tight and crying together, this really was the end now. I looked up at him and took one more look at his face.

"You are handsome though," I said as I wiped away tears, and he smiled.

"Say if in ten years time, I had money and a really good job that I'd trained for, and my own business, and a big fancy car, and I was doing alright for myself, had my own home and everything, would you get back with me?"

I looked at him and I shook my head, wiping the rest of my tears away.

"No, I wouldn't."

We both got in our respective vehicles, and we drove off, going opposite ways. It had been a sad but relieving day. Not the sour relief of our first break up, but the kind of relief that leaves your chest feeling lighter, and your head a little dizzy. And I am so glad we left on good terms. I think we both had compassion for one another and it felt better for me this way. I had lived out my karma, and felt ready to start anew. All I can say now is that karma definitely gets you. It has made me realise to only treat people with respect, ask for what you want, and to treat others as you would like to be treated.

My parents went back home to Spain and I was alone again. I was single, independent and for the first time ever, I was holding my own hand. I lived for my kids and they kept me going.

I am, and always will be, very grateful for these two people that came into my life, because without them I would not have my beautiful children, nor would I have experienced love, and I thank them for making me stronger as a woman. They helped to push me in a direction that I am obviously born to live this life for.

Part 3: Kim

13 GROWING PAINS

Christmas was getting nearer, that season of twinkling fairy lights and dazzling shop displays that looms eerily over every parents' bank accounts. It was cold and I felt very lonely, a lonely soul, but not quite on my own. I didn't have much energy or passion for anything. I had never been totally alone before, having always had family and a partner; it felt weird that I'd be spending the season on my own. What would happen to my kids? How would this affect them? I felt bad, and I had an urge to want to meet someone else to fill the void. Maybe I could go out with the girls to a club or a Christmas party and meet a new guy? I felt sorry for myself, even though it was my choice to be alone, maybe because everyone is a couple at Christmas, and I'd be left out looking awkward. I didn't realise at the time that I needed time out, time to myself to get to know who I really am, and what I really want.

I didn't even know who I was or what I was capable of, I had no goals or dreams, I had always just plodded on, getting on with whatever the day brings to me. I wanted to lose some weight; I had to start to at least make an effort. Even though my cheeks were gaunt, my small frame was carrying quite a bit of extra fat. I had ballooned in the past year, and I needed motivation somehow, but I had no energy, I couldn't be bothered and I was low, lonely and tired. I tried my hardest to put on a fake happy smile for the kids, and my brother and his wife, because they were all I had to comfort me. I carried on working at the supermarket, with hardly any paint jobs due to Christmas and I was still over indulging on the booze.

I told myself I needed the booze, it was keeping me chilled and stopped me from focusing on my worries. I couldn't focus on anything when I was intoxicated. I still thought another man would take my mind off of Joey, thinking I needed another man, but no one showed up. I was feeling needy, I needed hugs and affection, I needed attention and I needed to feel loved. I would spend most of my time in my daughter's room drinking and listening to the radio.

One hungover afternoon, I had been lazing around the house all day going through some things, when I came across a disc I had thrown into my top drawer. The disc read *"The Secret"* and I remembered that this was something that my sister had sent me from Australia

I had thrown it in that drawer the day it arrived and hadn't even thought of it since, though I suddenly felt the urge to watch it. I turned to my daughter and asked if she'd like to watch it, she said yes so I slid the disc into the TV and got under the covers.

At first I didn't believe it, but I was oblivious to science of any kind, especially Quantum science. It was too complicated and didn't make sense. We're all made up of energy? To me, gas and electric was energy, or if you're tired or feeling lazy you have no energy. I was ignorant to it, but by the end of the film I was in awe. *If this is real, then what the hell have I been doing to myself for forty years?* I got extremely upset with myself, I let myself get emotional about it, although I was emotional about absolutely everything back then. I would cry at the drop of a hat due to my circumstances and my drinking habits. Things had to change, but I had no idea how.

I had the radio on all the time, flicking through different channels, hearing nothing but sad songs, which in a way were comforting, because that's how I felt, like my radio knew which songs to play to match my mood.

I had to start to think positive, I had seen The Secret and it gave me the idea to pick up that book I had tried to read before, that positive thinking book by that lady who resembled my mum and sister. I found it and I read it again, taking notes this time and re-reading it over and over until it began to sink in.

It gave me the bug, I had to look at other books on this positive thinking stuff, did they all say a similar thing? They all have a similar message but are explained in different ways, because we all understand in different ways. It put me on a path, a fantastic journey, but I couldn't even realise it at the time. I had started something now; this was the beginning of my new beginning, my new life.

So in my notebook, I started to write down some goals that I wanted to achieve for the new year, 2011 was creeping ever closer and I wanted to lose a bit of weight, I wanted to give up drinking, I wanted to earn more money and maybe start the paint work as a proper legal business. I had been painting on and off but not really making a profit, and I wanted to start a computing course, I knew nothing about PCs or Word or Office, I didn't even know how to copy and paste.

Mid-December was when the snow began to fall, it was lovely, crisp and white and untouched in the dark of the early morning. I had always complained about the snow and the cold weather in winter, praying for summer and wishing my life away, but now I could see the beauty in it. It was calm and quiet; thick and pure white, our street looked stunningly beautiful, nobody was around and it was unspoiled. Its beauty made me excited, and for the first time ever I wanted to go out in it and enjoy it, like a child.

So I climbed up into the loft and scrambled to try to find my big black furry moon boots that my sister left for me, having no use for them in Australia, as well as my thickest coat and gloves. My daughter and I got all dressed up lovely and warm and set off out into the snow. We walked to the nearest park, standing around the back of the houses and we just had fun jumping about, making snow angels, having snowball fights and singing silly songs. We even videoed ourselves being silly on our phones, it was fantastic. It felt really good to be silly and make the most of the snow before it melted, I remembered The Secret had told us to have fun and to laugh and to radiate these vibrations out into the universe, and it will bring more of that back to you, so I was trying my hardest to feel good and laugh. It was great to be with my daughter, we hadn't had this much fun together for years.

My baby girl, I had neglected her, I had been blind, all wrapped up in my worries and woes and challenges and problems and my boyfriend, the time had flown by so fast, it had never occurred to me that she had grown into a beautiful, independent woman in her own right. I promised I would never do this again with my kids. I would always be there for them whenever they need me, I would support them no end.

A few weeks went by and one night my girl came home upset, she had split up with her boyfriend, she decided they were taking each other for granted, so she called for some time out, she told him not to ring her, not to contact her in any way, and he was to respect her wishes, she needed to think and decide how she felt and the alone time was important. They had been together from the age of fifteen and now she was nineteen. He did ring her, and she was extremely annoyed, but he was obviously hurting. I didn't interfere because it was her life, her partner and besides, me and him were still not talking. But I was there for her, I didn't take sides, I just observed, she was being so strong, their first break up, I know deep down she loved him, and I felt so proud of her, she noticed a bit of a lapse in their relationship and she said something, she communicated, something I was afraid to do in my relationships.

All too often we all take one another for granted, we seem to forget our priorities and what's dear to us, we sometimes forget to show love, and it all goes out the window, and then resentment can set in if we sweep things unsaid under the carpet. Communication and respect is the key; so in my eyes my girl was showing her concern for their relationship. After a few days they got back together, and she later told me that he thought he was going to lose her, and he was so scared he had to call, he couldn't bear to be away from her for a whole week. They sorted it out, they talked it through, and he fought for her, if a man loves a woman that much then he will move mountains to get to her. They communicated, and they still do.

At the supermarket, I had transferred to the cash office department, counting all the stores money. It was a stressful job handling all that money, counting every penny, it took hours, and when the machines were broken we had to count by hand. It was soul destroying but I had to start looking at it in a different way, at least I had a job, at least I had an income, I could pay my bills. I saw my friends and we had a laugh while we got the job done. I had a more positive outlook on life than I'd ever had before. I had to stop stressing that I was starting work at such an early hour, I had to learn to adapt by going to bed earlier and getting enough sleep, at least starting work this early gave me time to be able to paint furniture for more income when I got home. I had to learn to be grateful for what I had.

I had learned that researchers had been looking at how holding on to stress and worry and anxiety can contribute to and cause disease. When we stress our immune system shuts down and we are then open to disease and illness. I knew when I stressed and worried I had nothing but cold sores and flu symptoms and I felt like crap all the time, my body couldn't cope. Knowing this made me realise that I had to keep calm, and not worry so much and focus on other stuff, the stuff that's right in my life, I also had to keep telling myself over and over, *everything is going to be just fine, it's all going to work out right, it's okay*!

I began to notice signs coming to me more and more. When I worried and stressed out about stuff, I would sometimes hear Bob Marley on the radio, singing to me *"Don't worry about a thing, cus every little things gonna be alright."* Honestly, when I first became aware of this I was in shock, like the radio was talking directly to me! I kept this my secret, I didn't want anyone to tell me this was a coincidence, or that I was mad, but it did the trick, it kept me calm.

I had decided to clear out the loft, I really wanted to get shot of my old life and now I was on a mission. I got rid of everything connected to my old life; I even found the ring that Joey gave me for my birthday. I saved it from the skip, took it to a local charity shop and gave it to them; *at least it will fetch money to help the charity* I told myself. I began to find more and more things up there that I hadn't seen in years, stuff that I had stuck up there when I was with John, which stirred up a few unsavoury feelings, but I powered through. From up in the loft everything went tumbling down the stairs and by the time I had managed to clear all the junk from my staircase and living room, I felt as if a huge weight had been lifted from my shoulders.

I was becoming aware that there is more to life than the blind existence that I had been living, I was closed, fearful and unaware of how big this universe was, but I was becoming more and more open minded to it all. I felt like I was beginning to wake up and smell the coffee, I felt privileged and overwhelmed by it all. Being able to look at life through a completely different lens after forty years is an almost indescribable experience; it felt like I was seeing the world for the first time again.

I was begging to feel a bit better about my life ahead, I had some paint jobs from one of my first clients, and she had been pleased with my work so she called me back. I hadn't seen her for a few months, and she had a chair for me to shabby chic in antique cream. That morning I had been to a free networking meeting trying to get some contacts and maybe some work. I knocked on the door of her new bungalow and she opened the door.

She stood there with her mouth open and began screaming at me in disbelief. I looked smart, I supposed, from the meeting and I had a bit of make-up on. Usually, she had always seen me scruffy and covered in paint, no makeup and wearing old overalls.

"This is a new Kimmy!" she shouted with tears in her eyes, and she hugged me hard, and I couldn't stop laughing. Wow, she had got emotional about it, and I started to well up too. "Oh my God," she said, "you look so well Kim, you look different!" That said it all to me, I must have been a right state before, in her eyes she must have seen me as a poor little woman who had nothing, and I was. I was beginning to change and others were noticing; I was looking up instead of down. I had been down to the bottom, the furthest I could go, and now I had a chance to help myself back up.

I had some spare furniture that she had given me, which I had painted, and I drove it around to a few shops to try to sell it but no one was interested, so I decided to give it away to Saint Francis hospice. It felt good to help others and to give something back. It was a good warm feeling to give and expect nothing in return. She was the best client I had, she gave me the break I needed, and she passed me around all of her friends and family and kept me in work. I'm eternally grateful I knew her.

I was beginning to be very grateful for what little I had, I had never been like this before, since being on my own as a single woman. I started to appreciate myself and my life so much. I appreciated nature, my family and my loved ones. I was showing more love, hugging more, looking at people in the face and noticing them, I was texting my family telling them that I loved them, to which a few of them responded asking if I was okay. I really felt happy to be alive for the first time in years. I was beginning to realise that my parents were older and was questioning how long I had left with them. I knew that they were abroad, but at least I now made an effort to text or ring them until they came to visit me again. I noticed and thought deeply about the world and wondered why I was really here in this fantastic, miraculous world that I blamed whenever something went wrong. Now I know that we must all take 100% responsibility for our own selves and our lives. What happens to us is what we have subconsciously asked for or attracted to us, I understood that once we take on the responsibilities we can be a lot less angry at the world.

I looked at our planet, the solar system, the sky and its ever changing colours, nature, animals, insects, flowers and the seasons, the amazing humans that populated it. I began to realise that we must look after it, and work towards peace always. This life we are given is a gift, it's a miracle, and it's our journey. We're not here for long, so I decided I wanted to make the most of the second half of my life, with the knowledge that only I can change me.

I see us as a spirit or a soul living in a borrowed vessel, and I promised myself to keep my spirit alive while I can. *While I'm here, I will try to keep happy and be kind to others, because I know like attracts like, I get more of what I focus on and it will come straight back to me.* In The Secret, it says that you can cosmically order what you want from the catalogue of life, so I wrote down a new man, a new relationship, but this time I was specific in what I was asking for. He's kind and generous and loving, loyal and healthy with a stable job at least. Even though I knew I needed more time alone to find myself, I was still craving a relationship because I felt so lonely.

About a week before Christmas I went out with the girls to a club and I was so excited. I was thinking that maybe I might meet somebody. When we arrived, every man I saw had untrustworthiness about him; that was my mindset. I was not going to trust anyone I came across, I cast them as all being the same, *all men are the same, they all cheat, probably got wives and girlfriends at home and they're just out cheating.* I had to get out of this, because it was an old mindset, of course all men are not the same. And I was probably really radiating "back off" vibes anyway. So I just drank myself stupid and danced away.

The next day I had to deliver about 1500 catalogues in my area. I had taken on an extra job for more income in preparation for Christmas, so, hungover, out I went into the crisp afternoon air in my freezing cold van. Trundling around the streets in my giant, metal ice cube, it gave me time to think, *I wasn't meant to meet anyone last night, I'm too needy, and I'll only attract someone who's needy as well, if at all?* The perfect partner would come to me at the right time, when I wasn't even looking for a relationship, most likely. The radio kept playing a song by Florence and the Machine called *The Dog Days Are Over.* The song told me that the bad days are over and my new life is starting, which, even on one of the coldest days of the year, delivering catalogues in a cold, broken van, was something I believed wholeheartedly.

It snowed again just before Christmas day, and my daughter and I went to the park again, back to the top of the hill and shouted at the top of our voices all the things that we were grateful for, and all the things that we wanted. I wanted to be happy and she wanted more snow so that she didn't have to go to work that night. We laughed, and it felt good to be in the park in the snow. The next day I had to be in work by 5am, and believe me, it's bloody hard getting up in the freezing cold at 3.30 to get ready for work. I jumped in the van, a piece of toast hanging out of my mouth, as the engine began to fizzle to life, before sleepily falling silent again. A few more frustrated attempts and it still wouldn't start. I sat there for a while and thought about it, *I either ring for a cab or I phone in sick, but that meant no pay...*

I called the breakdown service and rang in sick, I had a hangover anyway.

The kids went to their dad's that Christmas Eve. I said it was okay for them to wake up with their dad because I knew I had a family to go to, and John didn't see his family that often. This would be the very first Christmas Eve I'd spend without my kids with me, and it was horrible, so I got drunk and fell into bed feeling sorry for myself.

I woke up Christmas Day, my head fuzzy from all the drink the night before. The cold outside seemed to permeate the walls and leak into every crevice of the empty house. The kids came back to me in the morning to open their few presents I had for them, and then they went back to their dad's for dinner. I quickly escaped to my brother's, not wanting to spend too much time in a cold empty house on a day that was meant to be about warmth and family.

14 OLD HABITS DIE HARD

The New Year came and went in a loud bang of greens and reds and yellows and blues, fizzling out against the starless sky, like a blank slate ready for me to really start over in the coming year. We all got drunk and the possibilities for what I could achieve in the next twelve months were endless and exciting.

I needed to step it up a gear this year, it was a new year, and I wanted it to be my best yet. A new chance, a fresh start, and I knew I had to put myself out there; I needed to ignite the light inside of me like a firework. I needed a drastic change, because if you carry on doing what you're doing, you'll just get more of what you already have, and I was sick of what I already had. My drinking, my job, how unconfident I was and my sadness, I'd had enough. It was only the kids who gave me a purpose; I had to be there for them.

I really needed to leave the supermarket job. I could train to go higher in the company, but it wasn't my passion. I saw and felt the stress of the people in the store who did climb higher to manage departments and the blood, sweat and tears of it all. No way was that my mission. I had my painting job that earned me a bit of money, but I needed to take that further and more seriously. It could be my chance, but my heart was still heavy and I was constantly tired.

I resolved to take my painting more seriously as a business. My daughter helped me set up a website, my very own website; I was excited and felt like I was finally taking some positive steps toward my future. I spent a lot of time in my room alone, doing a lot of thinking and listening to radio stations, to see if I could hear any messages. I'd write down my visualisations; writing one day: *I am a successful business woman, and I am sitting behind a large, expensive desk in a real modern building, I have staff to do all the admin work, I have a couple of inventions, that are a worldwide success and a highly acclaimed book. I have an entrepreneurial mindset, everything I touch turns to gold and I dress to impress, but on a Friday we have fun and dress in pink and purple.*

So I poured myself another vodka and dreamt of the future, thinking about what I wanted. I thought about my future soul mate, how did I want him to be? Is he sitting in his own space right now, getting drunk and feeling helpless and lonely and drinking to drown his sorrows like me? I knew that when I found him I wouldn't be a drinker, *I will be healthy and active and alive, and so will he.*

As much as I tried to be grateful, I had a hatred for my supermarket job now; I just couldn't see a way out of it. *I'll be there forever*, I began to think. It was getting to me big time, I had worked there for sixteen years and every bloody Sunday as well. The early morning starts were killing my sleep patterns, I kept thinking about when I did finally meet someone, and how he wouldn't stand for me having to cut Saturday nights so short. I was complaining and that gave me more things to complain about, and as usual my complaints came straight back to me, because you get more of what you focus on. I was focusing on what I didn't like or what I didn't want, which, guess what, gives you more of that. So I realised I just had to really try to be more grateful, I told myself and wrote down some affirmations, *thank you for my well paid job, thank you for the good people I work with, thank you for my income, thank you for my reliable van that gets me to work, thank you for my paint jobs*, and the list went on. I would visualise myself leaving the supermarket and being my own boss; running my own company. It took lots of practice and determination, I had to get out of being lazy minded and fearful of what could go wrong, I had to focus on what could go right, this was essential.

Things seemed to be picking up, the paint jobs were flowing in steadily, the money I needed was there, it felt good, I was saying my affirmations in the mornings and at night, I had them written on paper, a long list that I'd stuck to the wall so that I saw them whenever I was in my room. Making sure I repeated them every morning and every night.

I had been making a conscious effort to help myself and lose a bit of weight, I was over two stone heavier than I was a few years back, and it showed because of how small I am. I had started to go up into the loft and get on the air walking machine to get myself used to getting my heart pumping and active, my parents had left it to me and I was sure they'd be glad to hear that I was finally putting it to good use. So I would put my earphones in and walk and stride for forty minutes. I had it all planned out, once I started getting into an exercise routine, I'd be able to tackle my horrid drinking habit, and it'd all fall into place. It felt good to be able to exercise, after a while I started to think about my life and my goals, and what I needed to do. They say exercising is good for the mind because it relieves stress and helps you focus, and it was all beginning to come to me, I needed a business plan or something, I needed to write down what I want and say some affirmations to suit what I wanted. My dad had built me a small, wooden gazebo to work in, and attached it to my house. I used it to paint furniture in it but I was getting more phone calls and I needed more space. I had been networking quite a bit, and I had come across a lady who owned an upholsterers. We got chatting and she told me she had a space to let at her companies building. I told her I would think about it and at first I was doubting myself, I told myself *I have enough bills and stuff to pay out, how can I find extra money to rent space as well? Say if the paint jobs die down and I'm not so busy?* I forced myself to remember that you get what you think of, *stop doubting, Kim, and start taking chances, otherwise you will never know if you don't at least try, have faith it's going to be ok.* I had to switch my thoughts and look on the up side of life, and have faith that the Law of Attraction works.

I had been listening to a local radio station that covers all the goings on in my area, and they had started advertising a business expo that would be taking place not far from me, where you can hire a stall and advertise your business. I could take my business cards along, a few pieces of furniture and my portfolio along and see what happens, so I booked a stall. It made me feel good, I was taking action, I was becoming aware and using vision and inspired action and telling myself it would be okay, only good could come out of it, I have nothing to lose, and at least I'm trying. It felt good to get myself out there and stop the moping around, and the exercise was beginning to help me focus and think.

I took a trip to see the upholsterers and meet up with the lady I met at networking, she showed me around and she said I could leave a piece of furniture in the shop front for her clients to see, with a before and after picture on it, then she showed me the large space she wanted to hire out. The workspace was huge, I looked around and visualised myself working in there with all my paints and brushes set up on the side cabinets and the place filled with lots of furniture for me to paint. I got excited at the prospect, told her that I was very interested and that I would think about it and get back to her.

I left the place and drove away in my rattling, old van, and I couldn't stop thinking about it, it was in my head continuously, what I really wanted was becoming clearer and clearer to me. I saw myself building up the paint business from scratch, I could see in my mind how I wanted the room to be set out, and that I'd soon be driving a brand new, reliable van. I had work all the time and I could afford to leave the supermarket for good. Yes, this felt so good, being my own boss, no one ordering me around, I could hire staff if needed, bring it on. The ideas were swirling around in my head and making me feel great; then I extended those thoughts. *I could have so much spare money; I could go on holidays and treat the kids to whatever they wanted. I want a home in the UK and a home in the USA and a home in Australia near my sister.* It was difficult being on my own with two children to feed and all the bills and the mortgage and the debt of the credit cards. Honestly I don't know how I did it, but I tried my hardest and was beginning to trust in the Law of Attraction and myself.

I started to go out for walks at the park, just to get some exercise and fresh air, and to flush the paint fumes that sometimes got too much. Breathing in paint fumes while working gave me the same dizzying feeling I got after a good drink, but I wasn't about to poison my body anymore.

It was a lovely park, with lakes and hills and tracks. Various trees towered overhead and the paths went on for miles, to other towns a few miles away. Pure white swans and dragon flies drifted across the surface of the lake, and the air was alive with the electric buzz of passing insects. I was in awe at the beauty of it.

On my way to the park I had to pass a motorway. I always noticed vans, because I drove one myself, and I would always catch myself admiring a certain van that I was seeing a lot of, they seemed to be everywhere. I was noticing the Renault Trafic, it was bigger and longer than my van and newer as well. I visualised myself in one of those, I didn't care what colour, but I decided one day when I got home from my walk I would make a vision board of that van. Vision boards were something else that I had picked up from The Secret, and I was eager to try one out. A vision board is a tool you can use to help you to visualise what you want, some people say they find it hard to visualise or imagine things, so by having pictures of what you want looking back at you every day is easier than closing your eyes and imagining what you want. I got a large piece of card, and began googling images of Renault vans in all colours, in all positions, so that I could see all around it and even the interior of the van, and I printed them off, cut them out and glued them to the card. I did the same again with my painting business, I cut out paint brushes and decorating tools and pots of paint and images of ladies painting furniture and I made a second vision board. I proudly pinned them to my bedroom wall, where I could see them every day, and as I lay in my bed I would look at them and my imagination could run wild. *I am a full time business owner with my new, fantastic van and I am independent and happy and proud of myself.*

Six months had passed and I was still single; I had seen nobody that I fancied at all. Where were they all? At my age, most men are married, and my chances were slimmer now more than ever. It was times like this that I had to force myself out of my own mind, tell myself that I mustn't think this way, I was telling myself that there was someone out there for me, I just had to wait and he would show up eventually. I still had my trust issues to work on, and the barrier I had put up to protect myself from the breakup with Joey still stood, unmoving.

Being alone had given me time to figure stuff out and think about myself and what I wanted in life. It was just me now, my kids were young adults, and of course I would always be there for them, but it was my time now and I was able to finally discover myself after four whole decades. I could see what I wanted; I finally had some goals and dreams. I wanted to take opportunities and go for it now, just to see what happened, just try my hardest and trust the process. I had a bit more faith in myself because the words in the songs I heard were relating to me and what I was thinking. I had the overwhelming urge to want to help others and be the best I could be. I wanted to be kind, considerate and helpful, in any way that I could.

The biggest shock came to me via post one day, I was in my room as I opened a letter, the stamp on the front of the envelope told me it was from the government. I gasped as I read it. It told me that the vehicle I owned, my van, was an old model and it no longer met the requirements for the new laws that are to be introduced relating to the low emission zone in my area. I was shocked, they gave me a choice, I either get it converted to a low emission engine or I take the van off of the road, they also gave options of finance procedures to acquire other vehicles, but it all looked so expensive. The all too familiar feeling of panic wrapped its grip around me, *you have got to be kidding me*, was all I could manage. I didn't know what I was going to do, *how can I afford a van? I'm only part time and I just about get by*. It was giving me a few months notice, but I had to think about this one. My initial thought was that I'd just have to give up my paint jobs and work full time at the supermarket, and my hopes dropped to rock bottom again. *There must be a way around this*, I thought to myself.

I felt that I needed a break, I hadn't left the country for years, and the last time was in my thirties on a family holiday to Menorca with my parents and the kids. I knew I was in debt with my credit card but it allowed me more time to pay it off, and I thought of how much I would love to see my parents place in Spain. I wanted to see them so badly, so I booked the cheapest flight I could find, and I was excited, I had something to look forward to and it would take my mind away from my dashed dreams of a painting business, if only for a few days. We had such a good time at my parents' place, I hadn't realised how much I'd missed them until I saw them in person again. We laughed all day long, every day, and over indulged on the cheap local wine. The week flew by so quickly, and they confessed to me that they wanted to come back home to the UK because they missed the family and the grandchildren so much. My mum kept saying that she was low and missing her babies. I felt for them, but they had to at least try the adventure they'd asked for. My parents wanted me and my brother to visit them more but we simply couldn't take time from work and afford to keep on flying to Spain and back, to see them, they said they'd grown bored being out there on their own, and the Spanish government was not all it was cracked up to be, they had different rules in their country.

My dad found this a challenge. My mum was a sun worshipper and she was even bored of that, they wanted their family back, and they wanted to see the grandchildren grow up, they didn't realise it would be so hard. They missed everyone's love and hugs.

My face lit up, I would love them to come home, to have my parents back. I suggested that dad make a vision board of the UK and say affirmations about it, and he laughed at me, but I think he did ask, in his own way. As I was telling him I noticed a song that was playing on the radio, my ears picked up, the song was by the Stereophonics, it was called *Maybe Tomorrow*, and the words droned out of the tiny speaker: *Maybe tomorrow I'll find my way home.*

"Dad! Dad, listen to this song! Listen to what he's saying!" I urged. We listened to the crackly radio they had tuned into a station that played British music, my dad knew the song.

"Oh yeah! Oh my God, *I'll find my way home!*" We all started laughing, I was glad my parents heard that, it confirmed that it wasn't just me hearing messages from the radio. I proceeded to tell them about what had been happening to me, and the Law of Attraction, how amazing and weird it was all at the same time, but it gave my dad hope. My parents put the house up for sale and kept their fingers crossed.

I returned home from hot; sunny Spain and landed in the grey, miserable UK weather. When I got home I had four missed calls for potential paint jobs which really cheered me up. I woke up the next morning and my son had left me a note saying "*I love you mum*" and a single red rose lay beside it. I filled up with love and stood there and cried. *How lovely and thoughtful is that son of mine?* I was overwhelmed. That was the first time he had done something like that for me.

Negativity is a powerful force, though, and it didn't take long for me to get swept under by everything I had tried to escape when I went to Spain. I was still struggling with money and bills and being self responsible, only now I was doing all that with a tan. I found it a big challenge just to move from day to day sometimes, money and keeping a roof over our heads were my main concern, while my friends would pester me to go out, even though I could never afford it. It's not cheap to go out, so it was easier to stay at home and have a tipple of cheap wine to let my hair down. The numb buzz from the alcohol filled the void in my life for the night, until I'd sulk and flake out.

Around this time, I kept getting random phone calls from different companies asking for a Mr. Assaraf.

"No Mr. Assaraf lives here, now stop calling," I would tell them every time, though this went on for weeks and weeks. It was getting on my nerves, but they wouldn't stop. Even my daughter would pick up the phone and shout "He doesn't bloody live here, take our number off your system!"

One day she was watching The Secret in her room, and she shouted out to me out of nowhere.

"Mum, there's a man in The Secret called John Assaraf!"

I googled him and found out he had some books, so I scanned Amazon and came across his book "*Having it All*." I ordered it, a second hand version, which was all I could afford. Maybe it was a sign, I had it in my head now everything could be a sign, *be aware*, I told myself.

So I watched The Secret again, it's amazing what you pick up when you re-watch it, it explained everything I already knew, and what I wanted to do in my own life, but I was finding it hard to keep on trying to remember to apply it. I was continuously thinking about money, and worrying where the next penny was coming from. So far I was doing okay, but couldn't help the worrying.

The book came and I was eager to read it. In John's book he spoke about how if you give more, whether it's a service or money, then you will receive more of what you give. That seemed a bit difficult when you have bills and a mortgage to pay, but apparently I had to learn to trust in the power of the universe, *it works for everyone in the universe because it's a law just like the law of gravity, right?*

There was a lovely part in the book by a lady called Marie Ann Williamson, in which she says: "*Love is what we are born with, and fear is what we learn. The spiritual journey, (which is life) is the un-learning of fear and prejudice, and the acceptance of love is the essential reality, and our purpose on earth is to be consciously aware of it. To experience love in ourselves and others is the meaning of life. Meaning does not lie in things, meaning lies in us. No fear – no prejudice.*"

That resonated with me; I loved it and allowed myself to get emotional over it.

Re-watching The Secret and reading John's book had given me a new energy, I felt my faith in the Law of Attraction had been restored. I continued to work on my painting, knowing that if I asked for it, the universe would give me the business I wanted. One afternoon I was listening to my local radio station as I worked on my painting at home, singing to myself and feeling good because I had a paint job at the time, when the DJ announced a competition to win eight VIP tickets to a night club in town. The deal was to just text in your name, and if your name is announced then you ring the station and claim your tickets, simple! I wouldn't have even attempted to enter if the deal was to ring in and talk on the air, no way, I was nowhere near confident enough for that. So I text in and carried on singing in my good mood, imagining my friends and I all going out on the town courtesy of me and the radio station, and I felt really excited. A little while passed, and the radio had just faded into background noise as I concentrated on the dull, orange wardrobe in front of me, at the back of my mind I heard my name.

My ears pricked up and realised that my name was being called from the radio speaker on my window ledge. I was jumping around in my overalls, paint flicking everywhere, I was convinced that I must have attracted it to myself! I had been wishing in my mind for ages that I would be able go out and have a get together with friends, and it happened. I was laughing to myself, I couldn't believe it, I'd never won anything on the radio before. I called around to a few of the girls and told them, of course they were up for a free night out with free vodka and wine in the best club in town at the time. So we all went out, got too drunk, but had a great time. I kept promising myself to cut down on the drink for my own health's sake, I knew it was bad for me, I knew I wouldn't be able to lose the weight if I carried on, but I was addicted to a toxic substance that could kill me.

15 A UNIVERSAL LAW OF NATURE

The deadline with the van situation was looming ever closer, I had to take the van off of the road soon, and I had no idea what was going to happen. I was listening to the radio as usual, as the ordeal with the van was churning over in my mind; I was asking myself questions and I needed an answer. The radio had finished whatever song they were playing at the time and had changed to play the ads. They advertise a lot of businesses in our area, and they catch your attention by playing catchy jingles repeatedly. They began to play an ad that I'd not heard before, a cheery man sang about a local car and van dealer that specialised in Renaults. This advert was on repeat throughout the next few days, it seemed like they played it every half an hour all weekend. I looked at my vision board and I saw it, the Renault Van I had wanted so badly, the one I had been looking at every day and night, the one I had been wishing for, for ages, something in my brain pinged. *Get yourself down there girl, even just to have a look, just do it.* I had this sudden urge to go there, it was a lovely sunny day, and I felt okay. The bright sunshine helped my mood as I drove down to Romford towards the Renault Showroom. I pulled in, and parked up, there were cars everywhere, and a few vans, but they all seemed so expensive. I wandered aimlessly; disappointed and dejected over how expensive everything was, until young man walked towards me.

"Can I help you, madam?" he asked, politely. He was only in his twenties, very tall and pale; he wore a grey suit, and sported a kind face.

"Yes, I'm actually looking for a van, but these all look quite pricey, so maybe I'll leave it."

"Well what's your budget, we have a few deals that might be able to help you."

I just shrugged and told him I didn't know yet, because I still had to get rid of my old van first, and I proceeded to tell him about the low emission letter and all the trouble I'd had with it.

He smiled and said "We would be able to take your old van off of you as part exchange, let me show you around." I had nothing else to do so I followed him.

We walked all the way around to the back, and outside the showroom there she was. This gorgeous, deep cherry red, metallic seventeen foot, long Renault van, the colour made it look almost feminine. The immaculate metal seemed to twinkle in the sunlight, and I fell in love with it, I fell in love with a chunk of metal! It was exactly what I was looking for. My passion for wanting it was powerful, I just had to have it. The enormity of it seemed to dwarf my tiny figure, and I imagined myself at the wheel, looking down at everyone else on the road. He looked at me, and I was scratching my head, still in two minds as to whether I could afford it, but awestruck all the same. He asked if I wanted to go for a test drive, and I remembered that The Secret had told me that if there is something that I wanted, that I needed to get in it, view it, test it, and get the feel of it, so I said yes.

He drove it because I was not insured, but I was taking a good look around inside, at all the gadgets, the air con and the CD player, the plush interior and the massive, leather steering wheel, it made my old Peugeot look like an ice cream van. Wow, I could see myself looking professional in this, I was taking mental notes to myself, I really, really wanted it. We drove back and he told me I could pay it off in installments over 5 years, on HP or on finance, which gave me half a chance.

"I'm very interested, but I'll have a think about it." I said. I left with the biggest smile on my face, grinning from ear to ear with the vision still in my head, and I headed home.

The front of my home was a bit of a mess. I had a seven foot wide, black metal gate that I could just about get my old van through with a squeeze. I had scraped my van all up the sides trying to get it past the gates on to my drive, and to my right, I had three tall pine trees that had died, all brown and withered and unsightly. As I drove in, I wondered how I could have such a lovely van and probably end up scraping all the paint off?

Later, my neighbour knocked and we had a chat and a laugh over coffee, she told me her husband was in their garden cutting down their bushes with his new gadget, a chainsaw. My lovely neighbours had every gadget going; they were brilliant at home-making and DIY.

"I'd love to get my trees taken away," I said wistfully, "look at the state of them, I've been meaning to do it for ages." We had a hug and she left. Half an hour later she knocked on the door again, and to my amazement her husband was there too, chopping down my trees with his new chainsaw, and my eyes lit up.

"Thank you so much!" I squealed, and I flung my arms around her. "Oh my God! Thank you, thank you, thank you!" We were laughing, and I got emotional because they had come straight to my rescue. They just did it, there and then. All I could think now was *I have a bigger drive now, and that new van would actually be able to fit on it.* I was so excited, all week at work I was thinking of the red van, and on Saturday I thought *sod it, I'm going to take another look at it.*

I drove to Renault in Romford and I ordered the van of my dreams, it was there waiting for me. It was the most ecstatic feeling of achievement I had ever had; I was on my own, I was half self-employed, I was a woman who was standing on her own two feet, albeit completely petrified, but I trusted that it was all going to work out just fine. I trusted my own gut feelings; I didn't even focus on *what ifs.*

What if it all goes wrong? What if I can't afford it? It was all about *I can* and *I am,* I told myself over and over *I can achieve what I want, and I always get what I want, and everything goes right in my life, and I always attract the right people in my life to help me.* I was telling myself positive affirmations, and they seemed to work, if I wasn't meant to have that van, it would have been sold by the time I went back to get it, and if it had gone, then my attitude would have been, *oh well something better is coming for me.* My attitude was changing, because my thoughts were changing and I was getting results, I was getting somewhere, and it felt so bloody great. I was ecstatic; all I kept saying was thank you, thank you, thank you. I had never been that brave on my own before, but my determination kicked in, and I really surprised myself. I wanted something and I got it, even though I was left with the responsibility of keeping up the repayments, I told myself *I can afford this, I will easily earn this money.* The worst that could have happened was they would take the van off of me and I'd find another solution, but I erased that thought.

I now needed to step it up again and keep my mind occupied so I could cut down on the booze. I got on the internet, designed and ordered some business cards to get me going, and again, I started posting them around in affluent areas; all that walking meant I was even getting some exercise in, too.

Although it was tiring, I kept on going, though every now and then I would have a relapse or a few down days, and I would sulk to myself. The house would be such a mess and I'd live on beans on toast, which made me feel like a total failure. Soon enough, though, I'd come back around and start to think straight again, and then I would start to realise that I would only attract more of this to me, so I would imagine the life I wanted and pick myself up again.

I finally started to think about some goals I wanted to achieve, as I painted the furniture it was helping me to think; my mind was ticking over so I wrote down some aspirations.

I wanted to lose weight; I wanted to give up drinking or at least cut down, I wanted to exercise more and have more energy, I wanted to enjoy exercising and eat healthily, and I wanted to leave the supermarket for good. I wanted a clearer head so that I could expand my mind and focus, and become a better business woman. Most of all I wanted opportunities to help myself.

I remember quite vividly, Fleetwood Mac's song; *Don't Stop Thinking About Tomorrow*, playing on the radio a lot around this time. *Don't stop thinking about tomorrow, don't stop it'll soon be here, it'll be better than before, yesterday's gone, yesterday's gone.*

Don't stop. I wasn't planning to any time soon.

It was American Independence Day when I rented the upholsterers workshop for a whole week, which was great. I was so excited, it all went great and I felt important, like I was getting somewhere, the owners gave me a fantastic chance, and I was forever grateful to them.

I kept on seeing car number plates with WHU and West Ham related things as I began to spend more time outside, and later on I received an email invite to a women's business day in the West Ham football ground at Upton Park, so I booked it, without hesitation. Maybe West Ham signs were a sign that I should go to it, so I went, and had a great day. I gave out some business cards in the hopes the patrons wanted some furniture painted, and met interesting ladies with interesting jobs.

I was especially impressed by a young lady who spoke there. She was only in her late twenties, very smart and confident; she actually stood there on the platform and spoke for forty minutes in front of hundreds of business owners, telling us her story. I was so impressed, I had never been to one of these events before, I'd never noticed people's abilities before. I had to be inquisitive and learn from this, so that I could flourish, I was in awe of how confident she was; I thought she was so brave. *How can she stand there in front of a whole room and speak without being nervous*? I thought to myself. I didn't even have the confidence to put my hand up to ask a question! Her name was Mavis, and after I left, she was on my mind for days. I wished that I had walked up to her and shook her hand and told her well done for being so brave to a big audience. Within a few days I saw a car plate that read MAV 15, which said Mavis to me. I smiled when I saw that, and wished that one day I'd be as fearless as her.

With my paint jobs still not getting me anywhere substantial, I decided to go to St Francis hospice. I asked for the manager's name, and they gave me the contact details of a Mr. Rose. As soon as I got home I emailed and asked him if I could help the hospice with any paint jobs they might need doing, I had lots of time on my hands so I needed to be busy, otherwise I'd just slip back into the heavy drinking during the day. Mr. Rose emailed me back and we arranged to meet at his office; with my portfolio and all my samples in hand I headed over, and he was quite impressed by what I did. He told me that if any of the hospice's shops had any furniture they couldn't sell then he'd give me a ring and I would perhaps revamp them so that they could put them back in the shop, at a little higher price, and then we would split the profits. This seemed pretty fair to me, sharing the profit would at least cover the cost of the paint, even if I didn't earn anything, at least I'd be helping people at the same time. Some people couldn't understand why I was putting myself out to help others and, truthfully, I can see why they'd think that, I had no money for myself, and to be using the little I had on other people must have seemed ludicrous, but it made me feel good to help other people. I had my health, and an empathy for others who didn't, so why wouldn't I want to do something that was going to put some good out into the world? I worked for the hospice for a few months, having to leave when my paint jobs picked up at the end of the summer, and it was one of the most satisfying jobs I've ever had.

I would still get emotional over most things, some days wondering if this was it, if this was all my life was going to be. I didn't think I could carry on sometimes because I was so tired. I detested working at the supermarket, no matter how hard I tried, and no way was I going to go full-time there, I didn't want to fall into the trap of working there full-time and then I would have no way out, so I kept my hours there as part-time as was possible.

To cheer me up and numb my worries, I would treat myself to a glass of cheap wine every now and then. That made me even more emotional, especially when the soppy songs came on the radio. When I was feeling sorry for myself, I would text my family, telling them how much I loved them. At first my dad thought there was something wrong, that I was trying to sweeten him up because I wanted something, but I didn't, I just wanted to tell everyone how much I loved them. In my later years I have realised how much I love my family, and that I took them for granted for so long. I want to carry on showing them love like I never did before. I'm sure at the time they thought I was going mad, but I just felt empty and lonely, I wanted to show love and have love come back to me.

So, as usual, I poured myself a large glass of wine in the hopes of numbing the loneliness I couldn't shake; I was laying in bed, the children were away for the weekend. I looked out the window at the waxing moon, sipped on my glass of wine, and all of a sudden, I felt something spongy in my mouth. I quickly picked it out, and placed it on the side.

What was that in the glass? I thought. *I know the glass was clean, I checked it before I poured the wine, it had to have come out of the bottle.*

I switched on the bedside table lamp to get a close look, as the switch clicked and the orange light dimly illuminated the room, I saw something small and pink laying on the cabinet. I took a closer look at it, and it was a *maggot*, a maggot that had been dyed pink from the wine. I couldn't believe it, I nearly died! I had held pickled fly-spawn in my mouth. Flies carry disease and eat faeces and I'd held one of their babies in my mouth. I felt physically sick to my stomach. I dashed to the bathroom, emptied the remainder of my stomach into the toilet, and dumped the contents of the bottle straight after it.

Oh my God, that is a sign. I knew it was a sign for me to give that junk up, to this day I don't think I've ever been more disgusted.

I knew from then on I'd have to cut it out, and there was no way I was going near wine again, though at least with vodka I could see what was in the bottle. I continued jogging, or at least walking, wherever possible. Getting myself out in nature was something that made me so happy, especially in the summer. The walks helped clear my heavy head from the vodka the night before, and I needed to shift the weight that I hadn't been able to move so far. *Just try Kim*, I kept telling myself, I just had to at least *try*.

16 IF YOU'RE MEANT TO DO IT, YOU WILL

I had signed up to Sue Stone's newsletter earlier that summer, because I'd enjoyed her book, Love Life, Live Life, so much. Her website and newsletter were giving me so much positive inspiration against the stark, hopelessness of the outside world. Why would I want to be in a world like this? Sometimes I just wanted the world to stop, and I wanted to get off. But I loved her newsletters, they gave me hope for the world; I knew I wanted to be like her, I wanted to meet her and for her to infuse her positive magic into me. I continued to re-read her book, each time trying to absorb more and more, and trying to apply it to my life. What happened next was almost a waking dream, and completely changed the course my life was on.

I received an email from Sue, a standard newsletter that went out to all her subscribers. She was asking if anybody fancied being a life coach with the Sue Stone Foundation. This got my imagination going, and I thought about how fantastic that would be, and the thought made me smile. It would be so fantastic to help other people in their lives.

I can't even help myself, how am I gonna help other people? I thought.

Me being me, however, began doubting my capabilities, and telling myself that I could never do something like that. I had no qualifications or experience in this field at all. I told myself I was just a painter and decorator who worked part-time in a supermarket, how would I ever be able to do that? I was telling myself I wasn't good enough.

But, being a coach for the woman who'd changed my life was all I could think about.

A month later, the email was sent out again, but this time I read it properly. In the weeks leading up to receiving this email I had been hearing a lot of songs on the radio like *Stone in Love*, *Angie Stone*, *Papa Was a Rolling Stone*, and lots of Rolling Stones. Stone, stone, stone. She was in my radio and on my mind. My Reticular Activating System, the part of our brain that picks up on the things we are focusing on, was noticing anything to do with Stone, because it was in my mind. Our RAS will cause us to notice the things that we're thinking about, like when we find a pair of shoes that we really want, and suddenly everyone's wearing them. We attract more of what we focus on.

I took all of this in as a sign, and began to think that maybe I needed to investigate this more. Once I'd read the email again, more of what she was saying actually stood out to me. I hadn't read it in the beginning, but it actually said that there was no formal experience needed in this field, and that she would provide all the training personally.

Well, now I was thinking *oh my God, I'd love to take this further*, and I wanted to dig a little bit deeper. Perhaps this could be another way out of the supermarket; maybe I could even leave the low paid paint jobs.

I emailed straight away for an application form. *Okay*, I thought, *let's see what happens, it's only an application form, it can't hurt to see.* I was so nervous even sending the email. The application form came about a week later, and it was surprisingly easy. I poured my heart out on this application, and it all flowed out so naturally I actually needed more paper to explain everything.

There was one snag, I didn't have the money to pay for it. Obviously, this was a business and there was a charge, so I left the application form for a few days, I felt useless and crappy, wallowing in my own self-pity. I needed to change so much. After a few days, I was so upset I sent it, wallowing wasn't doing me any good and the worst that could happen was that I'd get rejected. I still wasn't ready to tell people about the signs I had been seeing and hearing. "What's happening to scatty old Kim?" they'd say. "She's going off the rails, she's drinking too much, what's she talking about seeing signs?"

I still struggled with the money and not being able to pay for the course. It was coming up to my daughter's 21st birthday, a special one, and I'd promised her that we'd all go out in London for a night out, as well as promising her some birthday money, because she was trying to save up as well. To my surprise I actually received extra tax credit in my monthly statement; I didn't even know about it until I looked at my bank statement and couldn't place where it had come from. This is what actually paid for Jeri's birthday, I was able to take everyone out, give her the money that I wanted to and even had a fair amount spare as well.

It felt like a miracle.

Soon after that, to my amazement, I received a personal email from Sue Stone. Not a standard newsletter, but a personal email, just for me. My stomach lurched as I read the name of the email, and I prepared to read her rejection. *Sorry Kim, but not this time*, it would probably say.

I read the email; my stomach flipping with every word. It said that she wanted to call me and have a telephone interview.

Me? She wants to speak to me?

This famous lady who was on TV and had a fantastic book wanted to talk to me.

I felt nervous straight away. My mind was filled with visions of heaven and clouds and angels, I cried in disbelief and told absolutely no one about this other than my own daughter. My own positivity started to kick in after that. *Think positive, think positive every single day*, I told myself. I was becoming more and more aware of the thoughts that I was thinking, and if they were negative I'd switch them around straight away. I started to think happy thoughts, envisioning my children's smiling faces, giving me lots of love because they were happy with their mum and they loved their mum and it was making me feel good.

And then the day came, the day that Sue had told me she was going to call. The interview was scheduled for that afternoon, and I spent the entire morning a nervous wreck. My house was immaculate from how obsessively I cleaned it, the tedium of housework managed to take my mind off of the interview for a few hours. I got myself looking okay; I even put makeup on, despite the fact that she wouldn't even see it, and started my new vision board. I allowed myself to be a bit more materialistic with this one, sticking cut out pictures of furniture that I'd like to own one day.

When Sue finally rang me she sounded so positive and so happy. My hands and feet were freezing cold from the nerves, but her voice was buzzing. She spoke as if we'd been friends for years, and, luckily for me, did most of the talking because I was too in awe to speak. Sue said that my application was amazing and inspirational, and that I'd make a great coach if I wanted to take part. I felt so grateful and overwhelmed and told her I'd love to be part of the team.

She continued telling me more about the organisation, that she had quite a few coaches who were dotted all around the UK and that she would love me to join the empire. The phone call only lasted about fifteen minutes, and when it ended I experienced such a high that I wanted to jump around the room just to get rid of all the energy!

Sue told me that the next stage would come when it was meant to, and as I hung up the phone, I heard a loud slap coming from the kitchen. I went to check it out and there in the middle of the floor was my vision board, flat on its face. I'd left it face up on the counter; there was no way it could have got onto the floor, because it wasn't standing up. How could it have fallen off the worktop by itself? Sometimes that still happens, there have been times when I've been thinking about my kids or my parents and their photos would fall from the corkboard in my kitchen to which they were pinned. Whenever I walk into a room and someone's picture is on the floor, it's always someone I have been thinking about, and I take these as a spiritual sign.

I started to gradually tell more and more people how to be positive, and I was getting more so myself, it seemed that the more positive I was the better a day I had. I was definitely a happier person after my interview with Sue, always thinking hard about all the good things in my life even when getting up for work at 3 am. I was saying thank you for my health and for the roof over my head and for my children and parents and loved ones. I could see what I wanted in my life; I could see my future and it was starting to feel really good.

I felt like I'd come alive, I was more alert; less comfortably numb. I stopped dreading everything and the days always ended great. My old sense of humour began to come back as I crept from my shell a little bit more.
I received another email from Sue Stone.

"Congratulations Kim! We would really love for you to become an accredited coach with the Sue Stone Foundation; you'll be our first Essex coach!"

I knew that this was all coming to me because I was happier. I had a chance to change my life, to help people become happier and more confident, to achieve their goals like I was starting to. It was like a dream to me.

I'd always been a listener, I'd listen to other people without getting in on the conversation, but to be a coach I would have to become a leader, now could I do that? I still had to get hold of the money and get hold of it before Christmas; I had no idea how it was going to happen and I remember feeling quite disappointed that I'd been offered this opportunity but didn't have the cash to do it. I tried to think of ways that I could get the money. Should I go to the bank? My family? Should I ask for more overtime? I was already starting work at 5am and then coming home to do paint jobs for my clients, which drained me, but I wanted to be a coach so badly.

I kept visualising myself on a stage, speaking to a room full of people. In my visions I was confident; smartly dressed with lovely make up and saying all this inspirational stuff to the audience, and at the end they'd clap. I could see the end result even if I didn't know just how I was going to get there.

I only had a few weeks to get this money; by now I was living in hope that another miracle would drop into my lap. Then it started to happen, the phone calls started to come in. Call after call after call for paint jobs, it was like a miracle. I thought everyone had gone mad, they all wanted their furniture done for Christmas, there were even large items and kitchens that paid a good bit of money. It kind of stressed me out a bit in the beginning, but I was buzzing as well, knowing that if this carried on I would be able to get all the money for the course.

I did it. Within weeks I had earned enough money to be able to pay the exact fee Sue was asking for. I was so proud of myself, I'd never earned this much money in such a short space of time before.

Even though it was December, I didn't even worry about Christmas, I was just so happy to be able to start my training in January. To feel happy was an understatement, my life seemed to be moving, I was finally moving on and it felt fantastic. I remember thinking to myself about how Sue had told me that if I was meant to be a coach, then the money would manifest and, oh my God, it did. I knew I was meant to do this.

Christmas came and went and I had a beautiful time with family and friends. I was so excited for January; I'd be getting on a train to Bournemouth and getting to meet the powerful lady herself. The woman I looked up to so much; who had dragged me out of my slump with a simple book.

KIM WYMER

17 A COACH IS BORN

My parents had come home for Christmas, and they dropped me off at the station where I would board my train to Bournemouth.

I was two hours early by the time I reached Waterloo station, I wasn't about to miss the train I'd worked so hard to get on. My train left from platform seven at 5:35 pm on the dot, and as the train pulled out of the station, I'm sure I could have looked back to see the old me had stayed behind. Hunched and miserable on the platform; watching the train pass her by. I wasn't that woman anymore, I had left her there on platform seven and I never wanted to be her again.

At Bournemouth station I hailed a cab that took me to my hotel. I set my alarm for 7am to get up early and have an early start. In the morning I walked from my hotel to the one where Sue was hosting the course. I began to feel nervous, but I couldn't stop smiling, every step I took was a step toward a brighter future, it was like walking in a dream world. I had attracted this to myself, I had taken control and taken action, I'd come out of my comfort zone and acted on an opportunity that had come to me.

I had to talk myself down from my nerves. I told myself that I knew how successful she was and all the things she'd done, but that she was just a person, just like me. *Snap out of it, Kim.*

There was no one inside when I arrived, so I sat on the plush sofa and took in my surroundings. The hotel was posh, fancier than anything I had ever been in, and from where I sat I could see the bar, hear the tinkling of its glasses and smelled the tiniest whiff of chlorine from a pool somewhere in the building. This was nothing like the cute bed & breakfast I was staying in.

Another lady arrived soon after; we looked at each other and we smiled,

"Are you here to see Sue?" we both asked, smiling and hugging each other. We were instantly on the same vibe of excitement and nerves; when we sat down she told me that she was an EFT teacher, which I'd heard of before but never really practiced and didn't know what it entailed. She proceeded to tell me that it stands for Emotional Freedom Technique, and quickly showed me a demo. I copied her and almost instantly I felt at ease, my nerves had calmed down completely and I felt more in control of my emotions.

We went up to the reception and asked for Sue Stone; the receptionist directed us to a room at the back of the hotel, it was a lovely big bright room with a couple of tables all nicely done with white table cloths, a coffee area and a large screen on the wall. As we walked in, Sue and her daughter, Natalie, were waiting for us.

The vibe in the room was so good, I felt like we'd known each other for ages. We took our seats around two large round tables as more people began to come in. When everyone had arrived there were only eight of us, all students of Sue's that had been hand selected by her. We proceeded with our training, which took all day and it was quite intense, there was so much information it was quite difficult to keep up. The course carried on like this for the next few days, and I felt like my head was about to explode, although we did have a good laugh at the same time, and Sue made it as easy as possible for us to learn. I still remember, however, thinking *how the hell am I gonna do all this*? This was intense studying and I was only a painter and decorator who worked in a supermarket. Then there was the business side of it, if I was going to do this I'd have to step out into the big wide world all on my own, pushing the limits of my comfort zone more and more and doing things I had no idea how to do. Not only would I have to coach one to ones, I'd have to stand up and speak for three hours on this stuff.

On the last day, we all got our certificates and accreditations, and it was one of the best days of my life. I had achieved something and I was now a qualified positive empowerment coach. We were given all the manuals, CDs and know-how, and Sue offered any help that we might need. We had pictures taken, which even went up on Sue's website, and a fabulous evening of dinner followed, with free flowing wine, of course. The butterflies were dancing in my stomach even as I stumbled back into my hotel room after way too many glasses of wine. I hopped in the shower and really started to think about what I'd just done. I was due home on the train in the morning, and it was up to me now, I'd been chucked out into the world with this qualification and what happens from now on is my responsibility. An overwhelming fear swept over me, self doubt seemed to cloud my brain, or was that just the wine?

I'd just trained with some of the most confident people in the world, most of them were teachers and coaches already, and were all used to dealing with clients. The teachers were already used to standing up and speaking; the coaches and personal trainers already had a handle on the business side of things, I seemed to be the most unqualified person in the room. I wasn't educated, I never attended college or university and only went to school to mess about and smoke in the toilets and now I was an accredited coach, I had to deliver this positive message to people. I stood in the shower, mulling it all over, and cried my heart out.

I was still crying when I got out of the shower, all the wine I had consumed wasn't helping me, and I couldn't believe that a trip I'd been looking forward to for so long would be ending on such a low note. My attention was drawn to the tiny TV in my room; as usual I'd just tuned it into some music channel as soon as I got back. On the little screen, Bob Marley was singing. *Don't worry about a thing*, his raspy voice warbled; *because every little thing is gonna be alright*. I wiped my tears away and allowed the happy tune to soak into my brain. This is what I was meant to be doing, I knew it, everything was going to be alright

I now know that there are no coincidences in life; I was meant to hear that song.

I woke up the next morning with a banging headache from the tears and the wine. Wine, I was addicted to the toxic shit and I wasn't sure how much longer I could take what it was doing to my body, no matter how good it made me feel the night before. I now had a new purpose; I would go back to my old world as a whole new person.

I knew what I had to do. I knew I had to create new business cards and a new website, practice my three hour speech *and* get myself some clients. I had to come out of my comfort zone, announce to everybody that I was a coach and not care if people thought I was crazy. For now, I would have to juggle three jobs and, looking back, it was not easy, this journey has been very tiring and back then I didn't even know where to start.

After pondering for a few days about where to start next, my nephew suddenly came to mind. He'd left college and there wasn't much work about for him, he wasn't feeling too good at the time and I thought that this would be the perfect time to test out my coaching skills on an actual person. It's so important that young people start off with a positive outlook on life, so he was the perfect candidate. After a few days of preparing what I would say, I went round to see him and we spoke for a good three hours; his feedback was pretty good and it made me feel good, but I knew I could get a lot better.

Next on the list was my website. I had to get myself a website and some business cards and, obviously, I tried the cheap online companies at first because you could do it yourself and it didn't cost a lot. I only knew the basics of computers so I had to work around this. I always doubted my abilities when it came to technology but I had to try, I kept telling myself *I know I can do it, I know I can*. Things had to change, as Sue says, there's always a solution, so focus on *that*, there is always a way around everything in this life. I remember, even as I was typing what I wanted to put on my website, inspiration was flooding over me. I got rid of my self-doubt because I knew it was the "*I am*"*s* and the "*I can*"s that really mattered.

As I went through the process of setting up my business, I wondered what I could call myself. I wanted to make people feel happier, more successful, and to not have any more miserable days. When I feel happy or when something's going good, I always say "happy days!" and that phrase seemed to fit what I wanted to do perfectly, so I called myself *Happy Days Coaching*.

The supermarket job had really worn me down by now, I had cut down on drinking a lot to allow me to really take my coaching more seriously but the early starts were the final block stopping me from fully committing to it. Every time I was in the office I would be asking the other managers if there were any other jobs in the store. I didn't want to start at 5 am anymore and I was willing to do any other job they had, but no managers wanted to help me, as if I were not meant to do it. So I decided I would transfer to a store closer to home, at least that way I wouldn't have to get up so early and travel, so I filled in all the application forms and called all the managers in the other stores but there was no luck. I tried and tried for a good few months only for every door to be slammed in my face.

I carried on giving a lot of free coaching to family and friends, and slowly, as good feedback came to me and I told myself that I could do it, my confidence was rising. I was getting out there and trying and I was doing it. I wanted to do so much because most of my life I'd held myself back out of fear of growing and changing, but I knew what to do now and it was up to me to apply everything I'd learned. The problems and challenges of life still came, and came in full force, but I was now able to deal with them in a completely different way. I didn't panic or worry, because I told myself that everything would turn out fine. I tried my hardest not to lose my temper or argue with my children, and to show love to everyone I met.

I had realised that love and health come before money, which is extremely important to understand, because if you haven't got health you can't enjoy the money, and if you haven't got love, all the money in the world will never be able to buy it for you. I'd realised what money was, just dirty paper; energy that flows in and straight back out again. Working in the cash office of a supermarket had really made me revaluate my relationship with money, seeing thousands and thousands of dirty notes all piled up in baskets to be counted. It was dirty and torn from being passed from person to person, yet it was the most important dirty paper in the entire world. I could never say, however, that having at least enough doesn't make all the difference, because it does, money may not buy you happiness, but it frees you from the constraints of the role society wants us to play, the dutiful worker. The most important thing to remember about money, however, is that you can't take it with you when you die.

As I knocked down every belief I had ever had, destroyed everything society had conditioned me to believe, I began to appreciate the supermarket a lot more. I became very grateful to the supermarket as my attitude changed, because it allowed me to earn money to pay for my food and bills. At least I had a job, was how I had to look at it, and I'd never seen it in that way before. I had to learn to love the people I worked with, because how could I judge them when I'm not perfect myself?

18 SEVENTEEN YEARS LATER

My life just plodded on, and the summer came and went, I was exercising more and more, and slowly but surely letting go of my need to drink alcohol. I carried on giving free coaching to my friends and family; every time feeling more confident than the last, and without the alcohol it became easier to remember everything I was teaching. I was looking and feeling better than I ever had before.

The months were flying by and I really wanted to give the supermarket job up. When November came around I took the leap of faith and decided to write my letter of resignation. I began trusting in myself and my abilities, telling myself over and over that it would all be okay, that I was meant to leave the supermarket and that I'd definitely survive on my paint jobs. Of course, everyone told me not to do it, they questioned me on how I would survive and if I was losing my mind, but they weren't the ones having to do this job, and I had to trust that my intuition was setting me on the right path. I typed up the letter giving in my notice, rereading it over and over; trying to pluck up the courage to hand it in. At the end of November the requests for paint jobs were rolling in, and it became a struggle to keep up with them and work at the supermarket, so I went in for my shift and handed my notice in, and I did it with a smile on my face.

I felt absolutely amazing, the weight of seventeen years in that place lifted in an instant, I felt free. I'd finally found the courage to jack it in. Some of my colleagues were shocked, and I'm sure some of them were jealous. I still had to do two week's notice, but knowing it would be the last two weeks I'd ever spend there made the time fly by. I knew I'd done the right thing; I didn't even entertain any thought that began with "what if?" I just focused on what could go right and what *was* going right.

Quitting the supermarket gave me the time to join some networking companies, and a friend of mine told me that she had joined a good networking company. What she didn't tell me was we had to stand up every week in front of everybody and talk about ourselves and our business for sixty seconds. I'd never stood up and talked like this in my whole life, and I was absolutely shaking in my boots. My friend and I were the only two ladies in a room full of thirty business men. I remember standing up for about thirty seconds, my voice wobbling and my hands and feet freezing, everyone was looking at me and I could feel my face going red. I was so embarrassed, and I sat down quicker than I got up. I felt shaken, and wondered how I'd ever be able to stand up and talk for three hours in front of a room full of people if I couldn't even do this for a minute. We had to do this every single week, and I'm so grateful to that company and my friend for teaching me to stand up and get over my fear.

I knew that in the New Year I was going to have to get a room full of people together, stand up and give this speech on positive thinking.

I decided I had to just book a hall, that way there was no backing out of it. *I'm gonna do this talk and test out my courage.* Mavis, the confident young woman I'd seen speak before came to mind, and I wanted to be like that so badly. I practiced day in and day out until the day came. All my friends and family supported me and twenty six people turned up to my very first talk. I was extremely nervous, and doing EFT left right and centre. My nerves took over and I spoke so fast that I'm not sure anyone actually heard me! I wanted it to be over, and when it was I couldn't believe that I'd actually done it, to stand up and give a talk on something I was so passionate about was a huge achievement in my life.

Leaving that hall my body must have been rushing with endorphins, and it gave me such a buzz that I wanted to do more. I was trying to arrange for myself to do another one, although I wasn't sure how I was going to get so many people together. At the next talk, I didn't have as many people, but I didn't care, at least if I was helping one person in the audience then I was doing my job, and I got some really great feedback.

I knew that I only had one month to go before I was going to sell my house, because the consent order had come through and said that I had to sell my house and give my ex husband the money I'd promised when my son turned eighteen. Then I would have money to play with to sort my new life out.

Whilst I was in the networking company, I met some really fabulous people, we had to see each other every week and we made a lot of friends. One of my friends there was an estate agent and I trusted him to sell my house for me and hopefully help me to find somewhere else to live, and a solicitor that helped me with the divorce procedure and the money exchange. By October 2013 I'd sold my house in Essex, where I'd lived for seventeen odd years. It was going to be fantastic because I no longer had to see my ex husband walking past my door every day. I'd seen him walk by nearly every day for the past seven years since we'd been divorced, and I was finally ready to move on. I didn't look at having to give him the money in a negative light, though that would have been a lot easier, I couldn't wait to give him the money because that way I was free and didn't have to be tied to him anymore. The future was positive and I was ready for it. I owed him absolutely nothing whatsoever anymore, and I was about to step once again into a new life.

So I wasn't a homeowner anymore, but this money would give me the opportunity to launch my brand new life and career. The painting business was very busy, and I was at the stage where I could have taken on staff, but I was ready to give up the heavy; dirty work of the paint jobs.

Some people told me I was mad to give painting up so soon after leaving the supermarket, but I didn't really care. I was happy to phone my accountant to tell him that I was no longer painting and had another new start coming to me. The extra money I got from selling the house allowed me to buy myself some new suits to match my new business mindset, I got my hair cut and indulged myself a little bit.

When it came time to move, I was adamant that I had to live in another three bedroom house, because I had grown so used to living in one.

My daughter came to live with me for a few months in my rented house, and my son chose to live with his dad. The rent was extortionate, three times more expensive than my mortgage, and after a few months my daughter and her boyfriend came across a lovely home that they wanted to buy. It came around so quickly that soon they were ready to move out, and she was ready to start a new life herself. Now it was just me left on my own in a three bedroom house with extortionate rent. I knew I would have to downsize before all of my money was wasted on a house that I didn't even need, so I contacted the estate agent and gave them notice to let them know I wanted to leave. I still kept positive, knowing that whatever place I moved to next was going to be even better than the place I was in now.

KIM WYMER

19 COMING FULL CIRCLE

One day I had a phone call from a lady that I'd never met before, she'd seen me on the Sue Stone website and wanted coaching from me. I was excited because it was my very first paying client, though I had not been prepared for what lesson the Universe had in store for me here.

We had arranged to meet and have the session at her house, which was beautifully extravagant. As I walked in I noticed a piece of classical music playing through the house, Beethoven's *Funeral March*. The lofty, sad tune gave the place a negative air; I felt almost overwhelmed by it. The lady told me that she loved classical music, and that this was her favourite song, a song she went on to explain was about death and grief. *Appropriate*, I thought.

We sat down and spoke for about two hours and as the session came to a close, I felt that I had done a pretty good job considering this was my first time coaching for money.

"Okay, payment," she said sharply as she slapped the money down on to the table. "So, do you think you were worth it?" she asked. I was floored! Was she playing mind games with me?

I felt embarrassed and had no idea how to respond, doubt began to take hold as I questioned if I was actually cut out to do this, maybe I wasn't worth it? I decided to take half the money for travel expenses and go. I felt instantly lighter as I made my escape, I knew that I'd just have to shake off the doubt if I were going to continue doing this. I knew I had to learn my worth and be more confident in the value of what I did. This experience had shaken me but I wasn't about to let that stop me.

That year I went to Glastonbury with some good friends, and we had a fantastic time. In a strange way, I felt like I had come home, though I was far from my real home, but the magical energy of the place gave me the strangest feeling that I'd been here before, I felt at peace. I bought some crystals and some candles and some books to help me learn more about spirituality.

I even had a past life regression, which was one of the more bizarre experiences I had there. I had a reading with the regressionist and though I couldn't scientifically back up why I said the things I did, somehow it resonated with me.

I felt that going there was really the start of my spiritual journey, it helped open my mind to the many weird and wonderful beliefs people hold and helped me appreciate my own spirituality more than ever.

In the spring, my daughter graduated from university, and after three years of hard work, she would finally get her degree. The venue was a lovely gazebo adorned with twinkling lights and littered with excited, educated people in gowns and hats; you could almost taste the electricity in the atmosphere. Of course, I knew my ex husband would be there, we hadn't spoken in years and my stomach flipped at the thought of how he might react to me. I knew he hated me because I was the one who had cheated on him and split the family up, but I couldn't miss the graduation over something like that.

When I arrived, I politely said hello to John, and to my surprise we actually spoke to each other! He had a little moan-up about the crowds of people, how badly organised he thought the event was and how nothing ran on time - every word that left John's mouth was a complaint and I almost couldn't believe it! It was so plain to see that the poor man had totally lost his way in his life, and the only thing he knew how to do, the thing he was best at, was complaining. I was laughing because he was being very witty, but I felt a very deep sense of sorrow, I wished that there was a way that I could help him. I wanted to tell him how sorry I was for everything that had happened in our past, to tell him about everything that I'd learned, but I knew it'd only be in vain.

He hadn't changed a bit, and still only believed what he chose to believe, so we continued with small talk until we went into the venue, to admire our beautiful daughter receiving her degree. We were both extremely proud; John was glowing with happiness. The atmosphere was so relaxed that he even opened up a little bit and he told me about a fantastic coincidence that happened to him. At the word coincidence my ears pricked up, if there was ever going to be a chance to tell him about the Law of Attraction it was now. He told me how he had seen a film the night before, and began thinking about how great one of the main actors had been in it, only to pick the actor up in his cab the next day. I knew this was my chance, so I told him all about the Law of Attraction and that he should look up The Secret online, which he said he would.

When the ceremony finished, we parted on polite terms, though I knew deep down that he still felt a lot of negativity towards me. I didn't see or hear from him again after that night, which didn't surprise me at all, but I knew we had been brought back together that night for a reason, and in a bizarre way it was even good to see him again, to come full circle back to the man who, in all honesty, had triggered this journey to a better, happier place. Only this time I had faced him as a totally different person. I was a happy, confident woman, instead of the meek girl I had been when we first met. I had finally shed the years of doubt, regret and fear that had held me back for so long, and now, the future stretched out ahead of me, bright and clear as glass. I still had a long way to go to get where I wanted to be, but I was alive and happy, which was, and still is, all that mattered.

EPILOGUE

In the amazing year that followed, I accomplished so many things in both my business and personal life, met so many people that have been sent to me to help me along my journey, and loved every minute of this beautiful life I've been given. I no longer fear public speaking as much as I used to, although the odd nerve still sneaks up on me now and then, and I continue to push the boundaries of my comfort zone and allow myself to experience the amazing, fulfilling life I deserve. I have sky dived in aid of St Francis hospice, faced my fear of horses and even started taking riding lessons! I've been doing more speeches, hosting radio shows, writing for magazines, and taking every opportunity that has come my way.

I've loved, lived and laughed more in this past year than ever before, and I want everyone else to experience a life like this. I want people to be kind and generous to each other, to see the good in the people around them and not let it be overshadowed by the bad. Negativity is easy, it requires no effort and yet so many people can't see that while it may be easy, it'll kill your spirit like poison kills your body.

At the end of the day, what I want to emphasise most is the amount of power people have over their own lives. Mine is not just a story of transformation, but one of empowered transformation, where every decision I made; every change I underwent I brought upon myself. I couldn't start enjoying my life until I stopped blaming the world and everyone else for the things that happened to me and began to take self-responsibility. When we, as humans, are operating in this mindset we become empowered, because every change you make, even negative changes, are brought around by you.

I still have many plans for the future, both personally and professionally. It still amazes me every day, how the people I need to accomplish these plans come into my life at just the right time, always showing up when I need them most and not a moment earlier. It is this gift of empowerment that I sincerely hope you will be able to take away from this book, I just can't overstate how much a positive mindset will improve your life.

Of course, there is more to a good life experience than just positivity, and throughout my life I have been privileged enough to be able to get where I am today, while others have not been so lucky. Positivity is not a magic pill that will give you everything you want without putting the effort in, much in the same way diet supplements will not give you the body you want without exercising. Being positive isn't going to stop other people treating you badly if that's what they want to do, but it will change how you deal with them, how you relate to them, and ultimately how you move on and go higher in spite of all the obstacles put in your way. It is when we enter this frame of mind that we open the door to all the possibilities our lives have to offer, and if we understand the price we have to pay to get to where we want to be, we need only to reach out and take the opportunities that come to us and help us along the way.

ABOUT THE AUTHOR

Kim Wymer is a writer, positive empowerment coach and owner of Happy Days Coaching. After hitting rock bottom in 2010 she set upon the journey of delivering the message of positive empowerment to the masses.

Kim has written extensively on positivity and wellbeing and has given talks across London & Essex. She has inspired many with her powerful words and has helped countless people transform their lives in the past five years.

Visit **www.kimwymer.com** for more information about Kim, booking information and details for upcoming appearances.

Connect with Kim at facebook.com/HappyDaysCoaching and @Empoweringkim

47628048R00085

Made in the USA
Charleston, SC
14 October 2015